Pension Fund Politics

Pension Fund Politics

The Dangers of Socially Responsible Investing

Edited by Jon Entine

The AEI Press

Publisher for the American Enterprise Institute

WASHINGTON, D.C.

Distributed to the Trade by National Book Network, 15200 NBN Way, Blue Ridge Summit, PA 17214. To order call toll free 1-800-462-6420 or 1-717-794-3800. For all other inquiries please contact the AEI Press, 1150 Seventeenth Street, NW, Washington, DC 20036 or call 1-800-862-5801.

NRI NATIONAL RESEARCH INITIATIVE

This publication is a project of the National Research Initiative, a program of the American Enterprise Institute that is designed to support, publish, and disseminate research by university-based scholars and other independent researchers who are engaged in the exploration of important public policy issues.

Library of Congress Cataloging-in-Publication Data
    Pension fund politics : the dangers of socially responsible investing / edited by Jon Entine.
        p. cm.
    Includes bibliographical references and index.
    ISBN 0-8447-4218-X (pbk. : alk. paper)
    1. Pension trusts—Investments. 2. Investments—Moral and ethical aspects. I. Entine, Jon.

HD7105.4.P463 2005
332.67'254—dc22

2005015919

10 09 08 07 06 05 04   1 2 3 4 5

Printed in the United States of America

Contents

1

The Politicization of Public Investments

Jon Entine

Should public pension funds invest the assets of their retirees based on the political views of the politicians who manage them? Should personal morality and ideology, which vary dramatically across the country, influence public investments, including Social Security?

Traditionally, public investments have been managed according to strict fiduciary principles designed to protect American workers and taxpayers. That tradition is now facing challenge. In some states and municipalities, including California, New York, and New York City, elected and appointed politicians responsible for overseeing public retirement funds are embracing highly controversial social and environmental criteria to decide on which companies to invest in or publicly lobby against.

This is part of a wider movement known variously as "socially responsible" investing (SRI), social investing, or ethical investing. Only a few years ago, SRI was restricted to a relatively small number of activists, who screened personal investments to reflect their political and social beliefs. With roots in nineteenth-century Quaker religious principles and 1960s activist ideals, the SRI community has assembled an array of idiosyncratic investment filters to decide which companies to invest in. The central tenets of SRI are an agglomeration of often conflicting beliefs: an opposition to arms manufacturing, nuclear energy, tobacco and alcohol production, animal testing, genetic modification in agriculture, and manufacturing processes believed to contribute to global warming; support for labor, women's and gay rights; and a vague commitment to "environmental sustainability."

Stocks of public companies deemed to have unacceptable records on these issues are screened out. Corporations involved in heavy manufacturing and natural resources almost automatically are judged negatively as these industries, which often generate high paying jobs with excellent benefits, are considered environmentally suspect. Those corporations judged to have "progressive" social policies or "clean" environmental records—often technology, pharmaceutical, and financial firms—are positively screened in.

While the SRI movement was launched and is still mostly encouraged by social liberals, true believers across the political spectrum and those determined to reward favored constituencies have actively promoted social investing.

Social investing developed a small but loyal following during the bull market of the 1990s in part because the high technology, communications, and finance stocks favored by social investors temporarily outperformed the more prosaic stocks in the S&P 500. But when the stock bubble burst, the myth of the superior performance of SRI funds burst with it. During the past five years, as of May 2005, SRI equity funds have lost 2 percent of their value while all equity funds have gained 0.3 percent, according to Lipper, the mutual fund research firm.[1] This volatility has led savvy financial advisors to generally steer clear of social investing. SRI's financial footprint remains tiny—certainly comprising less than 3 percent of all investments, and a tiny fraction of 1 percent of mutual fund investing.[2]

Yet, despite its problematic record, SRI continues to attract considerable attention from the media and social activists. And in recent years, social investors and advocacy groups have allied themselves with union leaders and sympathetic politicians, introducing ideology into the management of public pension funds with a stated goal of more directly influencing corporate and public policy. It has been estimated that more than 20 percent of state and local government employee pension systems use social screens to guide their investment decisions.[3]

The Problematic History of Social Investing of Public Pension Funds

State and local government pension funds collectively hold almost $2 trillion in assets. Another $897 billion is held in federal retirement accounts.[4] These funds have fulfilled a very important role by providing for the retirement security of public employees. The vast majority are defined-benefit plans whose main goal is to provide a specific level of retirement benefits to approximately 15 million members, who include general government employees, teachers, police, and firefighters.

Until recent years, the management of these funds was almost exclusively left in the hands of professional managers with little interference from state and municipal treasurers and the other politicians who technically oversaw them. Few funds incorporated social criteria. Because equity markets are relatively efficient over time, money managers forced to draw from a shallower pool of stocks did not believe they could adequately diversify their investments. And although there were no formal legal constraints, investing using social screens risked violating accepted standards of fiduciary responsibility.

Public pressure to incorporate some social factors, including using funds to target economically depressed areas, arose during the late 1970s and intensified in the 1980s, during the international boycott of South Africa and the campaign to limit investments in companies doing business with the apartheid regime. The earliest social investing initiatives involving pension funds were often cobbled together during crises, with little appreciation for unintended consequences:

- In the 1980s, the Alaska public employees and teacher retirement funds loaned $165 million—35 percent of total assets—to mortgages in Alaska. When oil prices fell in 1987, sending home prices plummeting, 40 percent of the loans became delinquent or resulted in foreclosures.

- In 1989, in what may well have been an election-year bailout of a failing firm, the State of Connecticut Trust Funds invested $25 million in Colt's Manufacturing Co. after a lobbying effort to save jobs; the company filed for bankruptcy three years later, endangering the trust funds' 47 percent stake.

- In the late 1980s, the Kansas Public Employees Retirement System (KPERS), then considered a model of activist social investing, made a $65 million investment in the Home Savings Association that became worthless when federal regulators seized the thrift. All told, KPERS wrote off upward of $200 million in economically targeted investments.[5]

Olivia Mitchell of the University of Pennsylvania reviewed the performance of two hundred state and local pension plans during the period 1968 through 1986 and found "public pension plans earn[ed] rates of return substantially below those of other pooled funds and often below leading market indexes."[6] In a study of fifty state pension plans over the period 1985–89, Roberta Romano of Yale University concluded, "Public pension funds are subject to political pressures to tailor their investments to local needs, such as increasing state employment, and to engage in other socially desirable investing." She noted pointedly that investment dollars were directed not just toward "social investing," but also toward companies with lobbying clout.[7]

Because of historically poor returns, state and municipal experiments in social investing remained limited until the 1990s, when the coffers at some of the largest pension funds began to swell. Elected officials in New York, Connecticut, Minnesota, and, most notably, California began to dabble in asset allocation decisions, focusing in part on a growing list of social concerns.

Today the California Public Employees' Retirement System (CalPERS) and State Teachers Retirement System (CalSTRS), the country's most politically influential public pension system, together hold more than $300 billion in assets. That is an enormous aggregation of shareholder voting power, a fact that has not been lost on ambitious politicians. Beginning in the mid-1990s, CalPERS and CalSTRS flexed their financial muscles by demanding corporate governance reform, publicly excoriating companies they deemed to be poorly managed. By the late 1990s, they had begun setting aside billions of dollars for favored social causes. For example, in 1999 the two pension systems combined to commit $7 billion to a program they called Smart Investments to support "environmentally responsible" growth patterns and invest in struggling communities. However, as in the cases of Alaska and Kansas in the 1980s, there were no accountability provisions to measure the impact of the venture, let alone to determine its financial consequences.

In 1999, California state treasurer Philip Angelides helped persuade officials at CalPERS and CalSTRS, on whose boards he sat, to sell $800 million in tobacco shares. As Angelides said at the time, "I feel strongly that we wouldn't be living up to our fiduciary responsibility if we didn't look at these broader social issues. I think shareholders need to start stepping up and asserting their rights as owners of corporations. And this includes states and their pension funds."[8] Since California sold the tobacco shares, the American Stock Exchange Tobacco Index has outperformed the S&P 500 by more than 250 percent and the NASDAQ by more than 500 percent. That decision alone has cost California pensioners more than a billion dollars.

Despite that huge financial setback, California and other state and municipal authorities have accelerated their social investing activities in recent years, divesting in companies and industries loosely linked to toxic cleanups, tobacco production, climate change, and the use of genetic modification in agriculture and food. The movement was empowered by a 1998 Labor Department letter that made clear that socially screened funds could be included in qualified retirement plans.

The foray into social investing by CalPERS and CalSTRS, once considered leading corporate watchdogs, has highlighted the conflicts of interest that beset the management of public employee funds run by ambitious politicians and union officials. Philip Angelides raised more than eyebrows in 2001 and 2002 when CalPERS committed more than $760 million to two funds created by Los Angeles billionaire Ronald Burkle, who, with his wife, had contributed to Angelides's run for state treasurer. For his announced 2006 gubernatorial run, Angelides is now actively courting large labor unions, which are well represented in the management of the state public pension funds. Eleven of the thirteen CalPERS board members, including Angelides, have union ties. CalPERS president Sean Harrigan, who is also executive director of the United Food and Commercial Workers Union, was ousted from the board in December 2004, in part because of his attempts to involve CalPERS in a labor dispute between Safeway and the UFCWU.[9]

Allowing short-term political concerns to drive investment decisions has often proved problematic. New York State comptroller Alan Hevesi, another advocate of social investing, intervened during the 2004 presidential election when Sinclair Broadcast Group decided to air a controversial documentary about John Kerry's post–Vietnam War activities. Hevesi, a Democrat and sole trustee of the state's Common Retirement Fund, which owned about 250,000 shares of Sinclair stock, sent the company a threatening letter saying the airing of the broadcast could hurt "shareholder value." The criticism, subsequently joined by numerous apolitical independent money managers, sent Sinclair's stock plunging 15 percent.[10]

Organized labor, which has an estimated $400 billion invested in public pension funds, has begun to view those dollars as political capital. For example, in an attempt to create jobs in Ohio, activists in the state legislature, backed by large labor unions, are trying to force the Ohio State Teachers Retirement System to invest not less than 70 percent of equity and fixed-income trades with approved Ohio-based brokers, and no less than an additional 10 percent with minority business firms. Dubbed "Buy Ohio," the bill has provoked critical editorials from most major Ohio newspapers concerned about the circumvention of traditional fiduciary standards. Even some public workers, who were being counted on to back the measure, have come out against the bill, claiming there is not enough investing expertise among brokers in the state to handle multibillion-dollar portfolios responsibly and estimating potential losses at $180 million.[11]

Union supporters are using their pension-fund connections to marshal opposition to privatizing Social Security. Gerald Shea, a top lobbyist for the AFL-CIO, has warned the country's largest brokerage firms, including State Street, J. P. Morgan Chase & Co., Morgan Stanley, Merrill Lynch & Co., Barclay Global Investors N.A., T. Rowe Price Group Inc., Wachovia, and Charles Schwab, against supporting the Bush administration initiative. According to Shea, organized labor has "no intention of letting any of these companies get away with [supporting the president's proposal] while they manage our workers' funds."[12] Echoing the stance of organized labor, three trustees representing the New York City Employees' Retirement System sent a letter to a half-dozen investment banking companies demanding a review of their position on Social Security reform.[13]

The well organized union attacks roiled the boardrooms of the tightly knit financial community. The Financial Services Forum (FSF), an umbrella organization then comprised of the chief executive officers of twenty-one of the largest and most diversified financial institutions, had supported the president's plan. The public contretemps prompted two of its members, Waddell & Reed Financial Inc. and Edward D. Jones & Co., to withdraw from the FSF. The fractured FSF then moved to rescind its backing.[14]

The AFL-CIO's aggressive campaign has set off alarm bells at the Labor Department. Concerned about possible fiduciary improprieties, the department sharply warned the union that the Employee Retirement Income Security Act prohibits public pension fund managers from hiring financial advisers based on their views on Social Security legislation. "The department is very concerned about the potential use of plan assets to promote particular policy positions," Alan D. Lebowitz, a department official, wrote AFL-CIO's top lawyer. "Our primary concern is union pension money has to be used in a way that benefits the retirees. Anything beyond questions of performance is inappropriate," agreed Derrick Max, head of COMPASS—the Coalition for the Modernization and Protection of America's Social Security, a vocal supporter of private Social Security accounts. The union responded by saying it would circulate the department's rebuke, but claimed it was not in violation of ERISA guidelines.[15]

Although union members and social liberals have been most active in trying to use the pension system to promote pet causes, SRI has also caught the fancy of some conservative activists. Consider the debate over whether to buy stock in Walt Disney, which has long been a favorite equity in many liberal SRI portfolios. In 1998, the Texas legislature prohibited state agencies from investing in companies that own 10 percent or more of a business that records or produces music allegedly glamorizing or advocating violent criminal acts, illegal drug use, or perverse activities. The conservative American Family Association of Texas immediately targeted the state's $27.5 million holdings in Disney.

"We believe investing in a company like this is bad public policy," said Wyatt Roberts, executive director of the Family Association. "I don't think that the citizens of Texas like the idea of subsidizing the destruction of their own children through the Disney Corporation."

"I think we should be setting a good example for the children of Texas," added Dr. Richard Neill, a state board member from Fort Worth.[16]

Although Disney had already netted the fund a healthy 35 percent return when the controversy ensued, some board members were more animated by their personal ideological convictions than their fiduciary responsibility to pensioners.

A few politicians have begun gingerly speaking out against the risking of pension funds on political causes. "I don't think that we should be using the city's investments policies . . . to advance social goals, no matter how admirable those goals are and no matter how much I believe in it," said New York Mayor Michael Bloomberg, who is a trustee of the fire and police pension funds.[17]

But Bloomberg's stance may be quixotic. With politicians and union officials dominating the process of making investment decisions in employee and teacher retirement systems, the politicization of the pension-fund system will likely continue to grow in the years to come.

The Essays

Should we encourage public pension funds to boycott tobacco companies, natural resource firms that do not embrace global-warming initiatives, or firms that utilize genetic engineering in agriculture, even though a boycott would have no discernible impact on the operations or profits of these companies, but would risk devastating the returns of pensioners who often have little say in what's being done in their names? What are the legal and political implications of this newly energized effort to socially screen billions of retirement dollars—and perhaps inject ideological screens into the management of the Social Security trust fund?

The essays in this volume examine these timely issues. In "Social Investing: Pension Plans Should Just Say 'No,'" Alicia Munnell and Annika Sundén, who have written often for the Brookings Institution, puncture the claims of social investing advocates that ideological filters can improve performance and bring needed social reforms. Munnell, the Peter F. Drucker Professor of Management Sciences and director of the Center for Retirement Research at the Boston College Carroll School of Management, and Sundén, a research associate at the Center and a senior economist at the Social Insurance Agency in Stockholm, conclude that social investing is a bad gamble for pensioners and a violation of fiduciary responsibility by public funds.

Charles E. Rounds Jr., a professor of law at Suffolk University Law School, echoes these concerns but warns that current state laws provide few legal limits on pension funds from dabbling in social investing. He argues that only new legislation—such as strict fiduciary limits that would likely accompany the creation of private Social Security accounts—can protect pensioners.

Jarol B. Manheim, professor of media and public affairs and of political science at the George Washington University, puts the debate over social investing and pension funds in a broader political and ideological context. By his analysis, the social investment community and its allies manipulate power structure relationships, systemic changes in shareholders' rights, and proxy battles over corporate policy to push a narrow political agenda.

The contributors, whose political views span the ideological spectrum, conclude that using public funds to invest in social programs or targeting investments in local communities hard hit by social ills or economic dislocations may be a worthy cause to be decided upon by legislatures, whose representatives are subject to the vote of constituents, but they have periodically proved disastrous for public pension funds, which do not submit such decisions to the vote of their members. Pension funds, and perhaps the Social Security system, are being dragged into treacherous waters where political grandstanding or moral righteousness threatens clear financial mandates. Politicians have led themselves into areas where they lack expertise, especially when their proposals involve complicated questions such as the causes of global warming or the costs and benefits of genetically altered food.

Certainly, as part of their fiduciary mandate to maximize investment returns for their beneficiaries, pension-fund trustees have a right and duty to lobby for changes in corporate behavior that could result in better returns for their pension holders. But judging by the words and actions of some pension-fund activists, "shareholder value" has become a fig leaf to justify a range of actions that may damage, directly or indirectly, the retirement holdings of members, prevent potentially profitable investments, and muzzle debate on government reforms. By implicitly encouraging the belief that the intentions of a business can be judged apart from its economic impact, social investing often promotes corporate behavior that is neither socially progressive nor ethical, and may result in adverse consequences to stakeholders, including pensioners. The consistent underperformance by SRI funds in recent years only underscores the extra risk that pension funds assume when incorporating social filters to select investments. In many instances, social investing amounts to little more than gambling with other people's money in support of ideological vanity.

Notes

1. Joshua Albertson, "SmartMoney Fund Screen: Socially Responsible Funds," *Wall Street Journal*, May 17, 2005, D2.

2. Jon Entine, "The Myth of Social Investing: Its Practice and Consequences for Corporate Social Performance Research," *Organization & Environment* 16 (September 2003): 362; Alicia Munnell and Annika Sundén, "Social Investing: Pension Plans Should Just Say 'No,'" paper presented at the American Enterprise Institute, Washington, D.C., June 9, 2004.

3. Jon Entine, "U.S. Pension Funds, Social Investing, and Fiduciary Irresponsibility," *Ethical Corporation*, January 2004, 24–27.

4. Employee Benefit Research Institute, "Assets in Qualified Retirement Plans, 1985–2002: Revised" (Washington, D.C.: EBRI, September 2004).

5. Cassandra Crones Moore, "Whose Pension Is It Anyway? Economically Targeted Investments and the Pension Funds," *Cato Policy Analysis*, no. 236 (September 1, 1995).

6. Olivia S. Mitchell and Ping-Lung Hsin, "Public Sector Pension Governance and Performance," in *The Economics of Pensions: Principles, Policies, and International Experience*, ed. S. Valdes-Prieto (Cambridge: Cambridge University Press, 1997), 92–126.

7. Roberta Romano, "Public Pension Fund Activism in Corporate Governance Reconsidered," *Columbia Law Review* 93 (May 1993): 795–853.

8. Ricardo Bayon, "California Leading," *Environmental Finance*, September 1, 2002, http://www.newamericafoundation.org/index.cfm?pg=article&DocID=963, accessed June 1, 2005.

9. Roger Parloff, "Pension Politics," *Fortune* 150 (December 27, 2004): 27–32.

10. Trent T. Gegax, "Stolen Honor: Democrats Fight Back and Win," *Newsweek*, October 20, 2004, http://www.msnbc.msn.com/id/6293163/site/newsweek, accessed June 1, 2005.

11. See Ohio Police & Fire Pension Fund, "OP&F Unites with Ohio Retirement Systems in Concern Over House Bill 227," news release, November 19, 2003, http://www.op-f.org/news/default.asp?id=11192003, accessed June 1, 2005.

12. Tory Newmyer, "Social Security Critics Slow to Coalesce," *Roll Call*, January 31, 2005.

13. *Wall Street Journal*, "Pension Fund Blackmail," March 31, 2005, A10.

14. Marie Cocco, "Dirty Battle in the Social Security War," *Newsday*, March 29, 2005.

15. Edmund L. Andrews, "U.S. Warns AFL-CIO on Protests about Social Security," *New York Times*, May 5, 2005.

16. Mary Alice Robbins, "Group Wants Texas Schools to Dump Disney," *Morris News Service*, July 2, 1997.

17. David Hafetz, "Use of Pension Funds Faulted by Some: Critics Fear Pension Activism," *New York Sun*, July 22, 2004.

2

Social Investing:
Pension Plans Should Just Say "No"

Alicia H. Munnell and Annika Sundén

Current social investing initiatives are generally not effective. Even if they were, private plans should not be sacrificing returns for social considerations, and public plans should not be engaging in any kind of social investing at all. Unfortunately, after decades of avoiding it, public pension funds are increasingly considering one or more forms of social investing.

Social investing takes three primary forms: screening (either excluding "bad" companies or including "good" ones); shareholder advocacy; and community investing. By far, the most prevalent form is negative screening, whereby the sponsor excludes firms involved with tobacco, alcohol, or some other activity considered undesirable.

Negative social screens to rid portfolios of "sin" stocks probably have no impact on the targeted firm, as long as the marginal investor is available to purchase the stock. Moreover, if done perfectly—with full diversification and no politics—social investing does not affect returns to shareholders. Some analysts argue that losses may arise under some types of investment models, and others that social

---

The authors would like to thank James Lee and Kristen Richards for excellent research assistance.

investing actually produces higher returns. But for discussion purposes, careful social screening probably nets zero.

With zero benefits and zero costs, social investing is probably fine in situations where the stakeholder and the decision maker are the same, as is the case with some private plans. But with public pensions, where the decision makers and the stakeholders are often very different, striking errors have been made in the past when social considerations have entered into the investment decisions.

What Is Social Investing and How Much Is Going On?

Today's social investment movement began with efforts to screen out "sin" stocks—tobacco, alcohol, and gambling—in the early 1970s. Pax World Fund then extended it to include opposition to the Vietnam War and militarism in general by creating a mutual fund which excluded investment in weapons contractors. The practice later took off in the early 1980s in the wake of a major campaign to encourage pension funds and others to divest from corporations doing business in apartheid South Africa.

Positive screens for firms with good records on labor relations, employment policies, or the environment are a more recent development. Shareholder advocacy also has more recent roots and involves communication between the investor and the company—directly or through proxy voting—on social and corporate governance issues. Community investment was an early form of positive social investing, but one that has not grown significantly. It involves channelling capital to entities that are perceived to be underserved, such as local housing markets, small businesses, employers of union labor, or community agencies.

An assessment of the size and importance of the social investment movement depends on how the phenomenon is defined. The Social Investment Forum (SIF), a trade group of social investors, reports that at the end of 2003, mutual funds with social screens held $151 billion.[1] Table 1 presents the individual funds that are available to the public—that is, excluding union

TABLE 1

**INSTITUTIONS WITH SOCIALLY SCREENED MUTUAL FUNDS
TOTALING MORE THAN $1 BILLION, DECEMBER 2003**

Institution	Assets ($ billions)
American Funds	55.1
AARP	11.4
Pioneer Investments	9.3
TIAA-CREF	4.5
KDL Research and Analytics, Inc.	4.5
Scudder Investments	4.4
Baron Funds	4.0
Thrivent Financial Management, Inc.	3.0
Ariel Corporation	2.7
Third Avenue Management, LLC	2.4
Calvert Group	1.9
New Covenant Funds	1.6
Pax World Funds	1.3
Domini Social Investments	1.2
PIMCO	1.0
Total	**108.1**
Share of all socially screened mutual funds	71.6%

SOURCE: Social Investment Forum, *2003 Report on Socially Responsible Investing Trends.*
NOTE: Union and other client-restricted institutions not included.

and other client-restricted institutions—by the various sponsoring organizations.[2] The largest of these organizations was American Funds with $55 billion, consisting of Washington Investors Mutual Fund, with $46 billion, and the American Funds Mutual Fund. The American Funds website description says that these funds "may not invest in companies that derive the majority of their revenues from alcohol or tobacco products."[3] The other large funds shown in table 1 also tend to screen for alcohol and tobacco.

Taking the SIF numbers at face value, the total number of mutual funds with social screens accounts for 3 percent of all mutual funds—excluding money-market mutual funds.[4] But we have some concerns about the numbers reported. For example, one of the union funds we discuss below, the Boilermakers' Co-Generation and Infrastructure Fund: Project Finance, is reported by SIF to hold $6.8 billion. But, in fact, the Project Finance Fund amounts to only $300 million; the rest of the $6.8 billion is invested without any social screens.[5] Hence, the SIF numbers appear to overstate the importance of social investing in the mutual-fund industry, and the total is likely less than 3 percent.

The other way that SIF measures social investing is by keeping a list of so-called separate accounts, which includes those institutions that base their investment decisions at least partly on social considerations. Specifically, the list is supposed to include all assets that are "screened, involved in shareholder advocacy, or are directed to community investing."[6] However, determinations of what does and what does not belong on the list tend to be inconsistent and sometimes misleading.

We looked closely at two Boston entities on the list—State Street Global Advisers and Boston College. The presence on the list of State Street Global Advisers, which has $1.1 trillion under management and screens $90 billion, seems appropriate, as does the assessment of its social investments.[7] SIF includes only the $90 billion of screened assets and, in fact, reduces the total to avoid double counting funds reported elsewhere.

Boston College, on the other hand, which has an endowment of about $1 billion, does not screen for anything. The university has a one-page directive, prepared in 1981, that says it will look at moral as well as financial aspects of its investment decisions, and it did participate in the 1980s and early 1990s in the boycott of firms doing business in South Africa, but it has not screened a single industry, divested a single stock, or voted a single proxy in the past ten years. Boston College officials suspect they are on the list because they subscribe to the services of the Investor Responsibility Research Center (IRRC).[8]

TABLE 2
SOCIALLY INVESTED PORTFOLIOS, 2003 ($ billions)

Year	Mutual Funds	Separate Accounts	Total
1999	154	1,343	1,497
2001	136	1,870	2,006
2003	151	1,992	2,143

SOURCE: Social Investment Forum, 2003 Report on Socially Responsible Investing Trends.

Overall, when SIF adds up all the assets of the religious organizations, universities, hospitals, foundations, and public pension plans on its list, it reports $2.0 trillion in socially invested separate accounts—10.4 percent of the $19.2 trillion in assets under financial management, as shown in table 2.

This is an overstatement, because it categorizes as social investing the full assets of a fund or institution that screens for a single product. Such an approach may be appropriate in terms of marketing social investing products. That is, if an institution screens for, say, tobacco, it is clearly open to the notion of screening for other products or perhaps investing in a screened mutual fund. But in terms of its impact on financial markets, including the entire portfolio seems excessive. An entity with a $10 billion portfolio that screens for only tobacco, for example, which, as shown in table 3, accounts for a mere 1 percent of the capitalization of the Standard and Poor's 500, seems a little less deserving of being entirely included into social investing figures than one such as the Boilermakers' Co-Generation and Infrastructure Fund: Project Finance, which supports union employment by co-investing in the construction of power-generation plants that are then leased or sold to independent power producers, industrial companies, or the government. The measurement problem arises because social investing is treated as a dichotomous activity for classification purposes, and generally it is not one. In terms of its impact on financial markets, social investing therefore involves significantly less than the 10 percent figure reported by the SIF.

TABLE 3
"SIN" STOCKS AS A SHARE OF THE STANDARD
& POOR 500, YEAR END 2003

Company	Ticker	Price ($)	Shares Outstanding	Market Cap- italization ($)	% of S&P
Tobacco				**126,698,856,500**	**1.23**
Altria Group, Inc.	MO	54.42	2,129,000,000	115,860,180,000	
RJ Reynolds Tobacco	RJR	58.15	84,600,000	4,919,490,000	
UST Inc.	UST	35.69	165,850,000	5,919,186,500	
Alcohol				**50,442,138,243**	**0.49**
Anheuser-Busch	BUD	52.46	814,759,936	42,742,306,243	
Brown-Forman Corp.	BF.B	46.72	121,100,000	5,657,792,000	
Coors (Adolph)	RKY	56.10	36,400,000	2,042,040,000	
Defense Contractor				**142,074,580,000**	**1.38**
Boeing	BA	41.98	800,200,000	33,592,396,000	
General Dynamics	GD	90.08	197,700,000	17,808,816,000	
Goodrich Corp.	GR	29.69	117,600,000	3,491,544,000	
Honeywell Int'l Inc.	HON	33.26	862,100,000	28,673,446,000	
Lockheed Martin Corp.	LMT	51.40	450,900,000	23,176,260,000	
Northrop Grumman Corp.	NOC	95.60	183,100,000	17,504,360,000	
Raytheon Co.	RTN	30.04	416,200,000	12,502,648,000	
Rockwell Collins	COL	29.95	177,800,000	5,325,110,000	
Casinos/Gaming				**17,801,890,000**	**0.17**
Harrah's Entertainment	HET	49.48	110,500,000	5,467,540,000	
International Game Technology	IGT	35.70	345,500,000	12,334,350,000	
Total S&P 500				**10,285,452,000,000**	

SOURCE: Altria Group (www.altria.com); RJ Reynolds Tobacco (www.rjrt.com); UST Inc. (www.ustinc.com); Anheuser-Bush (www.anheuser-busch.com); Brown-Forman Corp. (www.brown-forman.com); Coors (www.coors.com); Boeing (www.boeing.com); General Dynamics (www.generaldynamics.com); Goodrich Corp. (www.goodrich.com); Honeywell International Inc. (www.honeywell.com); Lockheed Martin Corp. (www.lockheedmartin.com); Northrop Grumman Corp. (www.northrum.com); Raytheon Co. (www.raytheon.com); Rockwell Collins (www.rockwellcollins.com); Harrah's Entertainment (www.harrahs.com); International Game Technology (www.igt.com).

TABLE 4

SOCIAL INVESTING IN THE UNITED STATES BY
TYPE OF STRATEGY, 2003 ($ billions)

Strategy	Amount
Screening	2,143
Shareholder advocacy	448
(Both screening and advocacy)[a]	(441)
Community investing	14
Total	**2,164**

SOURCE: Social Investment Forum, 2003 *Report on Socially Responsible Investing Trends*.
a. Some social investing involves both screening and shareholder advocacy, and these amounts
are subtracted to avoid double counting

Prevalence of Various Approaches to Social Investing

Although the SIF data probably exaggerate the extent of social
investing, they provide a unique source of information on the typical approach to incorporating social considerations into investment
decisions. Table 4 shows that in terms of assets under management,
screening is by far the most prevalent approach. Only about one-
fifth of assets are involved in shareholder advocacy, and community
investing activity is even smaller.

In terms of the types of social screens applied, SIF provides
information only for mutual funds; no comparable data are provided for separate accounts. As indicated in figure 1, by far the
most popular mutual-fund approach to social investing is a negative screen for tobacco; alcohol comes in second. The majority of
funds (64 percent) use a single screen; the remainder are equally
divided between those with two to four screens (18 percent) and
those with five or more screens (18 percent).[9]

Having a clear idea of the extent of social investing activity is
important to the subsequent analysis, because the nature and
magnitude of social investing matter. The thrust of the following
argument is that negative social screens—the most prevalent form

FIGURE 1

MUTUAL FUND SCREEN TYPES, 2003

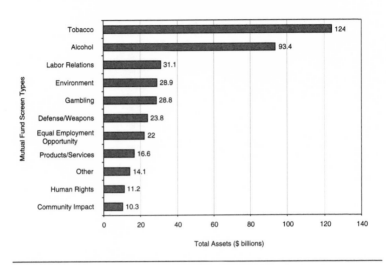

SOURCE: Social Investment Forum, *2003 Report on Socially Responsible Investing Trends.*

of social investing—most likely have zero financial impact on the targeted firms. At the same time, they probably cost investors little in terms of lower returns. The zero-impact, zero-cost conclusion rests on the assumption, which appears to be true, that socially invested assets are a relatively small share of the market.

How Does Social Investing Affect Companies?

Is the goal of social investing simply to make a statement against, say, tobacco or for, say, the environment? Or do socially conscious investors think they are going to affect the financial fate of the targeted firms? The SIF report suggests that social investing will indeed have a financial impact; social investors are putting their money to work in ways that will build "a better, more just, and sustainable economy."[10] The academic literature on the stock market, however, suggests the opposite; boycotting a stock is unlikely to have any impact on its price, because the demand for a company's stock is almost perfectly elastic. In other words, a relatively small change in quantity demanded for a stock—which has been shown to be the case with social investing since it accounts for an extremely tiny portion of total assets—does not significantly alter the price of that stock or the success of the targeted company. A couple of studies suggest that the demand curve may be less than perfectly elastic, but they are looking at sales and purchases that dwarf those involved in social investing. And a comprehensive survey on the effect of the South African boycott—the largest and most visible social action—documents virtually no effect, suggesting the real world mirrors the textbook model.

The Textbook Argument. According to standard finance theory, the price of a stock equals the present discounted value of expected future cash flows. Any significant deviation from the fundamental price would represent a profitable trading opportunity that market participants would quickly exploit and thus correct. As a result, the demand curve for a stock should be almost perfectly horizontal, and investors should be able to buy and sell large blocks of stock without there being a meaningful effect on the price. The shape of the demand curve is an issue whose importance goes well beyond social investing. Several basic propositions in finance rely on the ability of investors to buy any amount of a firm's equity without affecting the price.

Thus, the demand curve for a stock looks very different from that for, say, Chilean grapes—an item that consumers boycotted in the early 1970s to protest the coup by General Pinochet. The demand curve for Chilean grapes has a relatively steep slope, so a consumer boycott of the product, which shifts the curve to the left, results in fewer grapes sold and at a lower price, assuming an upward-sloping supply curve, as shown in figure 2. The action hurts Chilean grape growers and the Chilean economy.

In contrast, the demand curve for stocks is essentially horizontal. (The supply curve is vertical since in the short run the supply

FIGURE 2

SUPPLY AND DEMAND OF CHILEAN GRAPES AND THE
STOCK OF A GIVEN COMPANY

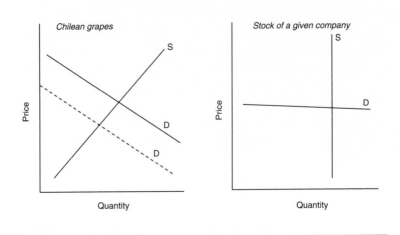

SOURCE: Authors' illustration.

of outstanding stock is fixed.) That is—in economists' terms—the demand curve is almost perfectly elastic. Elasticity measures the percentage change in the quantity demanded for each percentage change in price. If an item is relatively unique and has few close substitutes, the demand curve will be steep and less elastic. In contrast, if an item—such as the stock of a particular firm—has a lot of close substitutes, the demand curve will be relatively flat and more elastic. That is, a small change in price will lead to a big change in the quantity demanded. Or conversely, a big change in quantity demanded will lead to a small change in price.

The caveat is, of course, that potential buyers must not think the sale reflects a negative assessment, or the purchase reflects a positive assessment of the firm's financial condition or business prospects that could affect future cash flows. If potential purchasers believe the seller is disposing of the stock because he knows something adverse that they do not, they will lower their assessment of the stock's value, and the transaction will reduce its price. Thus, asymmetric information can generate steep demand curves where the purchase or sale of a stock is construed by others as good or bad news about future cash flows.[11] But if the transaction is not perceived to be based on new information, the demand curve for a stock should be virtually horizontal, and the price unaffected by any sale or purchase.

In short, the price of the stock is equal to the present discounted value of future cash flows. Boycotting tobacco stocks may result in a temporary fall in the stock price, but as long as some buyers remain, they can swoop in, purchase the stock, and make money. Thus, standard finance theory suggests that boycotting tobacco companies is unlikely to have any impact on the prices of their stocks.

Counterexamples. Because the horizontal demand curve is important to much financial theory, researchers have undertaken a number of studies to test it directly. At first, testing whether the demand curve for stocks is elastic seems easy—simply look at instances when buyers or sellers have traded large blocks of stocks, and see whether the prices have changed. A number of early studies took this approach and found significant price movements.[12] But the evidence is also consistent with the hypothesis that the sales or purchases reflected either bad or good news about the stock price. The challenge, therefore, is to find an event where the buying or selling has nothing to do with new information about the underlying value of the stock.

One such event is the addition or deletion of stocks from widely tracked stock indexes, and researchers have exploited this natural experiment. The first of these studies, which appeared in 1986, examined the change in stock prices when the S&P 500 announced it was going to add a company to the index.[13] From 1966 to 1986, between five and thirty-five companies were removed from the S&P 500 each year, usually as a result of takeovers. When the S&P removes a stock, it usually replaces it with another. In response, index funds usually purchase the new additions so that they can mimic the return on the S&P for their institutional clients. All six criteria for inclusion in the S&P 500—size, industry classification, capitalization, trading volume, emerging companies or industries, and responsiveness of the stock price to changes in industry economics—are well known, and none pertains to the future performance of the firm.

Nevertheless, this event study revealed that for the period 1976–83, the announcement of inclusion in the S&P 500 was accompanied by a 3 percent capital gain, most of which persisted for ten to twenty trading days. The study provided no information on what happened after twenty days. Several other papers have followed this approach and found somewhat larger price effects (about 15 percent) around S&P 500 index changes, most likely reflecting the growing popularity of indexing, from about 3 percent of the market indexed in the mid-1980s to 10 percent today.[14]

Two points merit consideration before applying these results to social investing. First, the magnitudes are very large. The index funds buy as much as 10 percent of the company's stock within a day or two of the announcement; we believe social investing amounts to only a fraction of that amount and does not occur instantaneously. Second, the experiment is far from perfect because addition to the S&P 500 may have implications for liquidity, the investor base, and financial health, which in turn affect prices.

Increased liquidity. Stocks in the S&P 500 are generally more liquid than those not in the index, probably because they tend to be bigger companies, enjoy a large pool of investors, and have a lot of information disseminated about them.[15] The liquidity is reflected in greater trading volume and smaller bid-ask spreads for S&P stocks than for the rest of the market. It would be rational for investors to pay a premium for liquidity because it reduces the likelihood of any adverse price impact when they sell the stock. If investors had been anticipating an adverse price impact from selling a less liquid stock not on the S&P index, then a liquidity premium could be capitalized into the price when the stock is added to the index. The effect could be significant.

Enlarged investor base. Another reason the addition of a stock to the S&P 500 might result in a price increase is a model suggesting that following the initial fluctuations accompanying the addition to the index, an increase in the relative size of a firm's investor base reduces its cost of capital and therefore increases expected future cash flows.[16] To the extent that the model holds true, adding a stock to the S&P 500 could increase its visibility to investors, make information more widely available, and open the stock to investors who might be limited to the index. The effect here is likely to be relatively small, however.[17] For example, one researcher who attempted to quantify the predictions of this model concluded that if 50 percent of investors do not hold a stock—that is, if the investor base is cut in half—the cost of capital for a company that constitutes 1 percent of a market portfolio will increase by thirty-two basis points.[18]

Endorsement effect. One could argue that the S&P 500 does not want to add the stock of a company that will shortly go bankrupt, in which case inclusion might have some informational value. Although the S&P explicitly states that inclusion in the index should not be construed as investment advice, it could still convey some positive information about the reliability of the firm. In this case, the endorsement effect that accompanies the addition of a stock to the index would be expected to have a positive impact on its price.

In short, while the S&P studies suggest that the demand curve may be downward-sloping, other factors—liquidity, investor base, and endorsement—could also explain the price response. Moreover, the magnitudes are enormous; index managers now account for 10 percent of the market. With that caveat in mind, it is useful to look at the findings from a study of the most visible and successful instance of social investing—the boycott to end apartheid in South Africa.

South African Boycott. In a 1999 study, Teoh, Welch, and Wazzan took a comprehensive look at how equity prices responded to sanctions and pressures for firms to divest their holdings in South Africa.[19] The conclusion that emerged from a series of event studies was that the antiapartheid shareholder and legislative boycotts had no negative effect on the valuation of banks or corporations with South African operations or on the South African financial markets. This is not to say that the boycott was not important politically, but merely that it did not affect financial markets. The study was organized around the sources of pressure for U.S. firms to divest: congressional action, pension funds and universities, and the individual companies themselves.

The bulk of the congressional action occurred in 1985 and 1986, when the U.S. government passed legislation imposing trade embargoes, currency sanctions, and lending restrictions. Most importantly, the Comprehensive Anti-Apartheid Act of 1986 prohibited new private or public loans to South Africa other than for humanitarian purposes. To test the impact of this prohibition, the study identified ten important legislative events leading up to the 1986 act and examined their effect on a portfolio of nine banks with South African loans. The results showed few significant effects on bank stock prices, and where significant they were positive rather than negative.

The purpose of the 1986 legislation was to hurt the South African economy, however, not U.S. banks. Therefore, the study then looked at the impact of the legislative events on, first, the largest South African firm, Anglo-American; second, two stock-based indexes, the Johannesburg Stock Exchange Gold Index and the Industrial Index; and third, the dollar/rand exchange rate. The effect on Anglo-American was significant in four cases, but the stock price increased rather than declined in response to the legislative events. Similarly, the gold index responded significantly for three of the dates, but again the sign was positive. The exchange rate responded negatively, as expected, to one House vote, but no other impact was evident. Thus, the U.S. legislative initiatives had no impact on a portfolio of banks or on the South African financial markets.

Pension funds and universities also put pressure on corporations. Pension-fund involvement in the issue began when a number of churches threatened to divest from banks doing business in South Africa. In 1977, the first iteration of the "Sullivan principles," which called for nonsegregation of races and equal pay for equal work, was adopted in the hope that by adhering to these principles, companies could continue doing business in South Africa and at the same time promote nondiscrimination policies.[20] But many felt the Sullivan principles did not go far enough, and in the wake of the continued controversy, Reverend Sullivan called in 1987 for companies to withdraw completely from South Africa. Many funds began to divest themselves even of companies that had followed these principles. For example, CalPERS divested itself of $9.5 billion worth of shares of companies holding South African subsidiaries. Pressure to divest and a worsening economic and political environment in South Africa led many companies (IBM, Exxon, Ford, GM, and Chrysler) to sell their holdings.

Teoh and colleagues looked at the effect of sixteen pension-fund divestments on a portfolio of firms with the highest exposure in South Africa. The results showed no evidence that the divestment announcements hurt firms with major South African operations. Analysis of the financial markets showed that, taken individually or together, the divestments also did not affect any of the South African financial indexes. Finally, the study explored how pension funds and other institutional holders of stocks responded to the divestment announcements. Here there was some mild evidence that institutional investors withdrew from pension funds before their divestiture announcements and returned when these companies announced their divestment.

But what happened to the stock prices of the individual companies? Three hypotheses are possible:

- Political or social preferences are an additional attribute in investors' evaluation of stocks. In this case, the demand curve would be downward-sloping, and regaining the approval of social activists—enlarging the investor base— would increase the firm's share price.

- Social activism that forces firms to leave South Africa causes them to forgo profitable investments and lowers their share price.

- Divestment has no impact, either because the two previous hypotheses balance or because the event is simply not that important.

The Teoh study looked at the stock-price effect of divestiture for forty-six firms, and found that the firms were neither positively nor negatively affected by the divestment announcement. Moreover, the no-effect result was not due to offsetting positive and negative effects. The likely explanation is that the boycott reallocated shares and operations from "socially responsible" investors to indifferent investors and countries. This finding is consistent with the assumption that the demand curves for stocks are highly elastic and so have little downward slope.

In short, the textbook assumption that the demand curves for individual stocks are infinitely elastic is a crucial one for much of financial theory. Because of its importance, researchers have undertaken a number of studies to test the hypothesis directly. A few suggest that the curve may be less than perfectly horizontal and that changes in quantity demanded could affect the price. But other factors could be at play, and the results depend both in theory and practice on the magnitude of the change and the size of the firms involved. The fact that an effort as large as the boycott of firms doing business in South Africa had virtually no effect on stock prices suggests that the financial effect of social investing on target firms is roughly zero.

How Does Social Investing Affect Shareholder Returns?

But does social investing affect returns to shareholders? Theoretical models of portfolio choice imply that restricting the portfolio to socially responsible investments could have a negative effect on the rate of return by limiting the ability to diversify. Given the large number of stocks available, however, the cost—using traditional asset-pricing models—is likely to be negligible. The bulk of the studies, which compare risk-adjusted returns for socially screened portfolios to those of unrestricted portfolios, support this claim.

Theory. Modern portfolio theory states that investors should diversify their asset holdings over a variety of securities. The gains of diversification build on the idea that the returns on all financial assets do not move in lockstep. An asset can be characterized by its expected return and the risk associated with that return, measured by the variance in returns. The risk of a specific asset can be broken down into two parts: risks that are unique to that stock (firm-specific risk) and risks that stem from market-wide variations, such as business-cycle variations, inflation, and interest-rate fluctuations (market risk).

When assets are combined in a portfolio, the return on the overall portfolio is given by the average return of the assets. And the risk associated with the portfolio is determined by the variance of the individual returns and the degree to which the individual returns vary together (covariance). Thus, by combining assets that have differing risk characteristics, an investor can create an efficient portfolio—one that is expected to achieve a given level of expected returns while minimizing risk.[21]

How many securities are needed for the portfolio to be efficient? Suppose an investor plans to divide his money among n stocks. According to Richard Brealey and Stewart Myers,[22] the portfolio variance is given by the formula,

Portfolio variance = 1/n * average variance + (1 – 1/n) * average covariance

As the number of securities in the portfolio increases, the contribution to total risk from the individual firm-specific risks decreases, and the contribution from covariance increases. Thus, as the number of securities increases, the overall portfolio variance approaches the economy-wide risk, represented by the second term in the equation. With two stocks in the portfolio, half of the overall variance is due to firm-specific risk and half to market risk. By the time a portfolio contains ten securities, 90 percent of its variance should be determined by the market risk. With a twenty-stock portfolio, 95 percent of the variance should be determined by the overall market risk.

Social investing implies that investments are based on considerations other than the tradeoff between risk and return. Portfolio choice is restricted by excluding "bad" companies or—less frequently—by including only companies that are following socially responsible policies. Screening securities could make it more difficult to achieve an efficient portfolio. But because an investor needs only twenty to thirty stocks to construct a fully diversified portfolio, the cost of a carefully screened portfolio is most likely zero. Eliminating tobacco stocks, for example, leaves enough securities to construct a market index; conversely, it is possible to put together an efficient portfolio from the full supply of socially responsible funds and companies.

Evidence. In the early days of social investing, studies pointed to the South Africa divestiture and argued that screening out stocks meant large losses. For example, in the 1970s, Princeton University reported that the stocks that had been excluded because of South Africa ties outperformed other holdings by 3 percent.[23] As time passed and researchers undertook more comprehensive studies, the conclusions shifted. For example, one study compared the performance of a portfolio free of South African investments to that of an unscreened New York Stock Exchange portfolio for the period 1960–83 and found that, after adjusting for risk, the portfolio excluding South Africa companies actually performed better than the unscreened portfolio.[24]

The positive results occurred because companies with South African ties were large, and excluding these companies increased reliance on small-cap stocks, which performed better on a risk-adjusted basis during this period. After adjusting for the size effect, the study concluded that effect of the divestiture on performance was negligible. During the late 1980s, the results were more mixed. On the one hand, the S&P 500 including South African stocks performed slightly better than the index without them, and one study of public pension plans found that South Africa restrictions had a small negative effect on returns.[25] On the other hand, in a 2001 study we analyzed data from the Surveys of State and Local Employees (PENDAT) from the early 1990s and found no significant effect on returns from restrictions on South Africa investments.[26] Thus, taking the period of the South Africa action as a whole, the conclusion is that its effect on returns was negligible.

In addition to the South Africa studies, other research has compared the risk-adjusted return of screened portfolios to the return of unscreened portfolios, while controlling for other factors such as firm size and industry effects. Most of the studies cover the period since the mid-1980s. Overall, the results show that the differences in risk-adjusted returns between the screened and unscreened portfolios are negligible and, in most cases, zero.[27] A few studies have focused on the effects of divestiture of tobacco stocks in the 1990s and shown that the risks and returns for the S&P 500 with and without tobacco stocks were almost identical.[28]

In addition to comparing the performance of screened portfolios to the S&P 500, several studies have examined the performance of social investment funds, such as those constructed by Domini and Calvert, relative to the S&P 500. The Domini Social Index includes 400 U.S. companies that pass multiple and broad-based social screens, and the Calvert Social Index is a broad-based index including 659 companies. The majority of the studies show that socially screened funds have no significant effect on risk-adjusted returns.[29] A few researchers have found that for subperiods, the Domini Index performed slightly better after controlling for market risk, size, and industry.[30] But the overall evidence supports the theory that the cost of carefully screened social portfolios is zero.

A recent study by Christopher C. Geczy, Robert F. Stambaugh, and David Levin challenges this view. The theoretical model for portfolio choice underlying the literature described above is the capital asset–pricing model (CAPM). Since the development of the CAPM, alternative asset-pricing models have emerged that associate returns with several independent influences, or "factors."[31] Furthermore, portfolio models do not say anything about how the skill of fund managers may affect returns and thereby the cost of social investing.

The new study claims that both these considerations—the assumption regarding the asset-pricing model and one's belief in the skills of fund managers—could affect the cost of social investing.[32]

Geczy and coauthors compared the risk-adjusted rate of return over the period 1963–2001 of portfolios consisting of socially invested mutual funds to an unconstrained optimal portfolio. Investors were assumed to make their investment decisions based on the historical returns of the funds, combined with their perceptions about the usefulness of various asset-pricing models and the skills of fund managers. The optimal portfolio was constructed for the same range of beliefs about asset-pricing and manager skill.

First, a portfolio invested only in socially responsible funds was compared to an unconstrained portfolio for an investor who believed in the CAPM and did not believe in fund managers' skills. The optimal strategy for such an investor was to choose a portfolio that closely tracked the market index. Restricting the portfolio to socially responsible funds meant this investor would simply choose socially screened index funds where the returns mimicked those of index funds without social screens. As a result, the cost in terms of reduced risk-adjusted returns was negligible; the socially screened portfolio earned only a few basis points less per month.

If the CAPM investor allowed for the possibility that managers of mutual funds might be skillful in implementing active strategies, the cost of following a socially responsible investment strategy increased. In this case, the investor would abandon the passive investment strategy by shifting from a diversified, index-style portfolio to an actively managed portfolio. The study found that this strategy increased the difference in returns between the unrestricted portfolio and the socially screened portfolio, and that the magnitude depended on how much faith the investor put in the managers' skills. For investors who believed in a 10 percent probability that a manager would add at least about 3.5 percent to performance, the cost of social investing was significant (about ninety-nine basis points per month).

The study also examined the costs of social investing if investment strategies were based on asset-pricing models other than CAPM. These alternative models implied optimal strategies quite different from the market-index tracking in the CAPM. As a result, the cost of restricting the portfolio to socially responsible funds when skill was precluded was about thirty-one basis points per month, compared to only a few basis points in the case of the CAPM. Alternative asset-pricing models raised the cost because it was more difficult to construct a socially responsible portfolio that mimicked the optimal portfolio.

Critics of the new study argue that other factors explain the results. The optimal portfolio under the alternative asset-pricing models included stocks concentrated in certain sectors that have performed very well over the past few years. The socially responsible funds, on the other hand, were broad-based, multi-industry funds, and the results could therefore be driven by differences in industry composition.[33] Furthermore, the optimal funds required large minimum investments and for this reason were not available to the average investor. Nevertheless, this study highlights the sensitivity of the "no-effect" results to the choice of the underlying investment model.

At the other extreme, some researchers claim that social investing results in higher returns because socially responsible companies are more successful than their less responsible counterparts. The argument is that policies such as the protection of the environment, good employee relations, and the promotion of product safety have positive effects on companies' performance.[34] For example, several studies have examined the effects of environmental policies. In one study of 243 stocks in 1991 and 1992, researchers concluded that environmental policies had a positive impact on the firms' returns after controlling for characteristics such as industry, firm size, and capital intensity.[35] Another study argued that good environmental management reduces firm risk and supported this argument by estimating the risk for 330 firms in the S&P 500.[36] Advocates of the "positive-return" hypothesis also claim that a socially responsible investment policy indicates a company has a skillful management and contend that companies with "good" boards performed better than those with "bad" boards.[37] Yet, other studies look at companies that are rated "one hundred best to work for" and conclude that they have superior performance.[38]

One problem with the "positive-return" studies is that it is difficult to prove which way the causality goes. It could be that profitable companies are the ones that can afford to be "good" simply because they are doing well, and that promoting socially responsible policies has no effect at all on performance. Thus, because these studies cannot distinguish between these two explanations, it is not possible to conclude that socially responsible policies have a positive effect on rate of return.

Another aspect that has received less attention is the administrative cost of social investing. It is possible that social investing is associated with higher fees and therefore has lower net returns because additional resources are required by fund managers to do the screening. The 2003 SIF report concluded that socially responsible funds appear as competitive as other funds when it comes to administrative costs.[39] However, others challenge this view by pointing out that some of the large-cap social index funds have above-average fees.[40]

To sum up, the vast majority of the empirical evidence supports the theory that the impact on risk-adjusted returns of a carefully constructed, socially screened portfolio is zero. Researchers have shown that social investing could have negative effects if investors believe in fund managers' skills. However, these results stem from comparing a broad-based, socially screened portfolio to a portfolio investing only in specific sectors, and therefore it is not clear that the results can be generalized. The studies that argue that socially responsible companies have higher returns because they are more successful have not been able to prove that the causality is not going the other way. Hence, the most useful assumption is that the effect of careful social investing on returns is zero, provided that it is undertaken with proper diversification and an absence of political pressure.

Should Pension Plans Engage in Social Investing?

The argument regarding pension plans modifying their investment decisions to reflect social considerations consists of several tiers. First, if the decision makers and stakeholders are not the same, pension plans should not engage in social investing because the tastes and incentives of the two parties are not necessarily aligned. Moreover, any deviation from maximization of return for a given level of risk is dangerous when activities are conducted in a highly political environment. These concerns make social investing particularly undesirable in public plans. Second, if the stakeholders and decision makers are the same, as is often the case with private plans, then costless—and most likely ineffective—social investing seems acceptable. But social investing that involves a sacrifice of return for other considerations should never be undertaken even by trustees of private plans. The reasons here are twofold. First, such activity may result in a significant lack of diversification on the part of plan participants. Second, the reduced return is equivalent to a tax-subsidized gift to the recipient of the invested funds, and while the tax code allows deductions for gifts to nonprofit entities, it has no equivalent provisions for gifts to profit-making concerns.

Public Pensions. Social investing is not a good idea for public pension funds. The decision makers and the stakeholders are not the same, and these plans have gotten into trouble in the past. Furthermore, recent stories suggest that investment policies are often still highly political. And the stakes are large. About 2,600 state and local pension funds hold about $2 trillion for more than 20 million public employees and retirees.[41] Assuming that most state and local plan assets belong to defined-benefit plans that provide a specified level of benefits to members (although a few states have added defined-contribution components), these assets exceed those held by private-sector defined-benefit plans (table 5).

Stakeholders versus decision makers. Retirement boards of elected, appointed, and ex-officio members oversee state and local retirement systems. The boards typically have between five and eight members, although one-third have between nine and eleven.[42] In other words, investment decisions are generally made by five to eleven people, including mayors, treasurers, comptrollers, city councilors, union leaders, and citizens. Restrictions generally take

TABLE 5

DISTRIBUTION OF PENSION ASSETS BY FINANCIAL
INSTRUMENT, YEAR END 2002 (percent)

Asset	State and local plans	Private Plans	
		Defined-benefit	Defined-contribution
Equities	51.0	43.0	37.8
Mutual funds	—	5.4	23.0
Bonds	18.4	14.7	5.1
U.S. Gov't Sec.	18.6	14.8	3.8
Cash	2.7	9.0	2.5
GICs	—	5.0	14.5
Mortgages	1.6	0.4	0.5
Other	7.7	7.7	12.7
Total	100.0[a]	100.0[a]	100.0[a]
Total assets (billions)	$1,963.8	$1,585.1	$1,947.5

SOURCE: Federal Reserve Board, Flow of Funds, 2003.
a. Totals may not add up to 100 percent due to rounding.

the form of the "prudent-person" standard, requiring that investments be made with the "care, skill, and diligence" of a prudent individual. In some cases, the prudent-person standard is supplemented by "legal lists" specifying the allowed types of investments and the maximum amount of assets that can be invested in certain securities.[43]

Despite the restrictions, the process is often conducted behind closed doors and subject to little public scrutiny. Moreover, many state and local plans are still run in-house and involve the selection of individual stocks rather than broad-based indexes. Although our perception is that investment practices have improved a lot over the past twenty years, scandals still arise. A recent front-page New York Times article reported that political money sometimes affects pension investment decisions. In the worst cases, pension trustees dole out investments not on merit, but on the basis of the money managers' contributions to an official's campaign. As a result, pension boards may overlook excessive fees or high rates of turnover and approve inappropriate investments.[44] In short, the decision makers consist of a small group of people who may not represent the will of the constituents, who operate under little scrutiny, and who may be subject to financial and political pressure.

On the other side of the pension divide are the stakeholders. These include current state and local workers, retired public employees, and tomorrow's taxpayers. The idea is that today's taxpayers make pension contributions on behalf of today's public employees to cover the cost of compensation for services provided; that is, accrued pension benefits are simply the deferred wages of public-sector workers. Although states and localities could always levy taxes to cover pension benefits in the future, it is sensible to put aside money for these benefits when they are earned, so that the taxpayers who enjoy the services pay the full costs associated with their provision.

These accumulated contributions to the pension fund are invested in an array of financial instruments whose success determines the funds available to pay public-sector workers when they retire. Since, as indicated earlier, state and local pensions tend to be defined-benefit plans, the amount paid to retiring workers is determined by a formula rather than by the holdings in the pension fund. Thus, to the extent that returns are inadequate, future taxpayers, who are not represented on the investment boards of the public pension funds, will have to contribute more to cover the cost of benefits.

In extreme cases, current and future retirees could also lose out. While it is unlikely their initial benefits would be cut, future legislatures facing a pension shortfall could reduce cost-of-living adjustments or cap the base to which these adjustments are applied. Current and future beneficiaries usually have only limited representation on the pension boards.

In short, investment boards of public plans should not undertake social investing because the stakeholders are unlikely to be involved in the decision making. Even simple screens may not be consistent with their interests.[45]

Lessons from experience. One reason to take a hard line with respect to public pensions is that they have engaged in social investing in the past and have been burned. In the late 1970s, some observers identified the large and rapidly growing funds in state and local pension plans as a means for achieving socially and politically desirable objectives. The initial debate focused on attempts to exclude from pension portfolios companies with undesirable characteristics, such as those with almost totally nonunion workforces or investments in South Africa. The focus quickly shifted to undertaking investments that would foster social goals, such as economic development and homeownership.[46] Advocates generally contended that the broader goals could be achieved without any loss of return.

Early reports, however, suggested that the targeting did involve sacrificing return. For example, a 1983 study of state-administered pension funds showed that thirty-one states had undertaken some form of targeted or social investment.[47] By far the most prevalent was the purchase of publicly or privately insured mortgage-backed, pass-through securities to increase the supply of mortgage funds for homeownership. Analysis of the risk/return characteristics of these targeted mortgage investments revealed that ten states either inadvertently or deliberately sacrificed return in an attempt to foster homeownership. The sacrificed return sometimes exceeded two hundred basis points. Although mortgages accounted for only 5 percent of total state and local assets, state and local pension funds were naïvely traveling a dangerous path.

In their initial forays into economically targeted investments, public pension fund managers generally did not appear to recognize the "Catch-22" nature of the exercise. For the most part, the goals of increasing in-state housing investment and maximizing returns are inconsistent in America's highly developed capital markets. Any housing investment that offers a competitive return at an appropriate level of risk, such as a Government National Mortgage Association (GNMA) investment, does not need special consideration by public pension plans, nor would such consideration increase the long-run supply of mortgage loans. Investments by pension funds that would increase the supply of housing funds must by definition either produce lower returns or involve greater risk. Sophisticated advocates of targeted investments recognized the efficiency of the market for housing finance and argued that pension funds could make a contribution through innovative forms of housing finance.[48] But that was not what was going on in 1983; the in-state mortgages purchased by public pension funds tended to be conventional, fixed-rate, thirty-year mortgages.

The losses in the early 1980s were a sharp wakeup call to a number of public pension fund managers who appeared to believe they could accomplish social goals without sacrificing returns. Over the past twenty years, the rhetoric associated with targeted investments has changed markedly. Public pension fund managers, sensitive to the potential for losses, go out of their way to make clear that they are no longer willing to sacrifice returns for social considerations; almost every definition of social investing includes a requirement that the investment produce a "market rate of return."

In 2001, we undertook a detailed study to determine the extent to which pension funds were engaging in social investment, and the answer was "not very much."[49] The study looked at all three avenues, discussed earlier, through which social or political consideration could enter the investment decision: community, or "economically targeted" investing, shareholder advocacy, and screening and divestiture.

Three separate surveys conducted during the 1990s suggested that economically targeted investing, which caused such a stir in the 1980s, accounted for a maximum of 2.5 percent of total state and local portfolios.[50] Pension-fund managers universally agree that it is improper to sacrifice returns for social considerations, and therefore look for investments that offer market return and provide collateral investments. Whether this is a useful exercise or not depends on one's view of the efficiency of markets.

In terms of shareholder advocacy, in 1998 public pension plans—primarily those of California, New York, and Wisconsin—accounted for 6 percent of the total shareholder proposals related to corporate governance.[51] In 2003, that share had dropped to

FIGURE 3

SPONSORS OF CORPORATE GOVERNANCE PROPOSALS, 2003

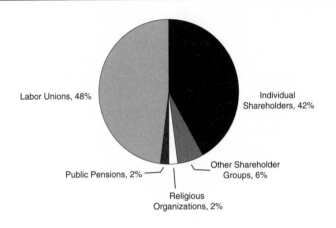

Labor Unions, 48%

Individual
Shareholders, 42%

Public Pensions, 2%

Other Shareholder
Groups, 6%

Religious
Organizations, 2%

SOURCE: Georgeson Shareholder, "Annual Corporate Governance Review: Shareholder Proposals and Proxy Contests," 2003, http://www.georgesonshareholder.com/pdf/2003%20a.wrapup.pdf (accessed May 17, 2005).

2 percent, with labor unions and individual shareholders dominating the scene (figure 3).

It is hard to evaluate the success of shareholder activism using survey data because so many factors affect the bottom line. Some detailed studies suggest some positive effects, but the results are somewhat sketchy. We found no effect on the rate of return. The main point, however, is that not much was going on.

Finally, the main story with regard to screening and divestiture is the selling of stocks in companies doing business in South Africa in the late 1980s. Public plans joined universities, foundations, and others in undertaking this action, although they did so reluctantly and late, and only after the "Sullivan principles" no longer provided an acceptable compromise. Also, as soon as apartheid ended, public plans immediately purchased previously barred stock. In the case of Northern Ireland, on the other hand, where anti-Catholic practices were being carried out by government officials, little divestiture occurred until the "MacBride principles" were set out in 1997.

Public pension funds also resisted pressures to divest tobacco stocks, even though other institutional investors began divesting in the mid-1980s. At the time of the 1998 study, Massachusetts, Florida, and seven other states had introduced restrictions on tobacco holdings; California divested soon thereafter. On the other hand, by 2001 Florida and Maryland had reversed their divestment decisions.[52] So the story appears to be that public plans resist divestiture and try to exhaust all avenues of compromise before taking such an action.

The conclusion from our 1998 survey was that public pension funds had learned their lesson about social investing. It was very difficult to find investments that paid a market return and produced additional benefits. Similarly, altering the portfolio in response to each political issue—Northern Ireland, Iran, Cuba, the Arab League—was not a sensible strategy. Finally, divesting "sin" stocks was to be avoided as much as possible. Public plans were on the right track; it would be a mistake for them to reverse course and pursue social positions.

Recent developments. The recent interest of public pensions in private equity investments raises a number of concerns. A decade ago, public plans had virtually no money in private investments; today, data compiled by Wilshire Associates suggest that private equities amount to almost 5 percent of public pension assets.[53]

One issue is that private equity investments have the potential to combine social investing with an exemption from disclosure. Apparently, some top-tier firms have rejected investment offers from public pension funds because the plans might be forced to disclose private equity information under state laws.[54] In response, the Colorado legislature recently exempted the $29 billion Colorado Public Employees Retirement Association from having to reveal information about its private equity or other alternative investments. In Illinois, a bill is winding its way through the legislature that would create a not-for-profit, venture-capital firm that would make investments in "underserved regions of Illinois"[55] and would exempt those investments, as well as the private equity fund investments of all public pension funds in the state, from Freedom of Information Act requirements. The tradeoff here is between the participation of public pension funds in deals with high returns and high risk on the one hand, and transparency on the other. If ever there were an area where transparency should be given paramount importance, it is public pension fund investments. Exempting public pension funds from disclosure is asking for trouble.

These private or alternative investments have also sparked an inquiry by the Securities and Exchange Commission regarding the role played by pension consultants.[56] Public pension funds rely heavily on the advice of consultants because fund boards are required to invest hundreds of millions of dollars but often have little financial training—only the largest can afford professional investment staffs. The problem is that the pension consultants have business relationships with both the pension funds and the money managers they recommend. It is not unusual for the consultants to host elegant gatherings for pension board members, and for money managers to pay tens of thousands of dollars to participate and meet the trustees—"pay to play." The resulting increase in money being guided into public pension plans raises a host of concerns. These investments may offer high returns, but they also carry substantial risk and often involve bigger fees than those applied to simpler, publicly traded investments. Because they are not publicly traded, it is much more difficult to evaluate their performance, and they cannot be sold quickly to raise cash. Although these private equity investments need not fall under the heading of social investment, they are troublesome in their own right and raise additional concerns when targeted to "underserved regions in Illinois" or comparable efforts.

Private Pensions. With regard to private plans, the question of social investing arises primarily in the defined-benefit arena, which accounts for $1.6 trillion of the $3.5 trillion of private plan assets. Defined-contribution assets consist mainly of funds in 401(k) plans, where the individual makes the investment choice. Since the 401(k) decision maker and the stakeholder are the same person, none of the agency problems arise. But individuals need to be careful, since 401(k) plans are not producing the magnitude of accumulations that were expected, and the assets are over-invested in company stock.[57] Note that private, defined-benefit assets are less than those held by state and local plans.

In the case of private defined-benefit plans, the decision makers and stakeholders are more likely to be closely linked. The exception, of course, arises in the case of bankrupt plans. Unlike in public plans, the Pension Benefit Guaranty Corporation (PBGC), an entity established under the Employee Retirement Income Security Act (ERISA) of 1974, insures the benefits of workers covered by private plans. The PBGC imposes premiums on sponsors of defined-benefit plans to insure workers against the loss of benefits if their plan terminates with inadequate assets. Thus, really bad investment decisions have the potential of burdening the sponsors of other defined-benefit plans. But the pool of potential stakeholders may be even larger, since the PBGC is inadequately funded should a number of large plans fail simultaneously. The question is then whether Congress would allow workers in bankrupt plans to lose their benefits, or whether it would turn to taxpayers for a bailout to cover the shortfall. Most observers believe the taxpayer would be on the hook. Thus, in extreme cases, the decision makers and stakeholders could be quite different. For purposes of discussion, however, assume that the sponsor is sound and termination is not an issue.

When the decision makers and stakeholders are the same, screening investments seems like a harmless activity. If employees of a hospital want to keep their money away from investments in the health-debilitating tobacco industry, so be it. As discussed above, such screening probably has virtually no impact on tobacco companies, but at the same time, it is probably a costless activity when it comes to returns.

But we would argue that anything more ambitious is not a good idea for two reasons—diversification and tax policy. Take the example of the Boilermakers' Co-Generation and Infrastructure Fund, which has been described as "one of most sophisticated and successful alternative investment programs."[58] This union fund uses a project-finance model to co-invest in the construction of power-generation plants that are then leased or sold to independent power producers, industrial companies, or the government. Over its first twelve years, the Boilermakers' Fund has invested $450 million in thirty projects and earned a 15 percent return on its funds.[59] Although the 15 percent rate of return equals that on equities, supporters claim that the Boilermakers' Fund takes less risk, since it provides just the senior or subordinated debt for each project financing and usually takes the lead in structuring the deal.[60] Since the goal of the investment is to ensure that the project employs union boilermakers, it also is reported that the Boilermakers' Fund has generated 1.4 million hours of work for its participants.[61]

Should private plans be engaged in this type of activity? Our view is "no." First, placing a significant amount of pension money in one business means that the pension trust is holding less than a fully diversified portfolio. (This is not a problem with the Boilermakers since the Project Finance Fund accounts for only 4 percent of total assets.) Such concentration flies in the face of modern financial theory, which says that diversifying a portfolio offers large gains at little cost.[62] It is even more important for workers to diversify their investments away from their employers. Concentrating pension assets in the industry where workers earn their living means that participants are concentrating their financial bets in an area that is directly correlated with their own human capital—that is, their earnings—which in almost all cases is their primary source of income.

The second issue in this kind of economically targeted investment is the potential for providing a subsidy to the lessees or purchasers of boilers. Although the returns appear quite high for industrial lending, which typically returns prime plus a couple of points, it still may be possible that the union is subsidizing the makers of boilers in exchange for using union labor.[63] To the extent that the union is subsidizing employers, it is equivalent to earning a market return and then making a gift to the boilermakers. While the union should be free to make the gift if it so desires, its members are not entitled to favorable tax treatment on that gift. Under the personal income tax, gifts to religious and charitable institutions are tax-deductible, but no equivalent deduction is available for gifts to profit-making entities. Making the gift through a reduced return is equivalent to taking a deduction for that amount. The favorable treatment of pensions under the Internal Revenue Code, which allows the deferral of taxes on pension contributions and earnings on those contributions until benefits are paid in retirement, was designed to encourage pension coverage and retirement saving—not to subsidize gifts to boilermakers or other employers.

In short, social investing has virtually no place in the pension world. In the case of public plans, the dichotomy between the decision makers and the stakeholders makes it unlikely that the two have similar tastes and interests. Moreover, diverting attention from maximizing return for a given level of risk in this highly political environment is asking for trouble. In private defined-benefit plans—with the exception of bankruptcy—the decision makers and stakeholders are more likely to be the same entities. Therefore, costless screening seems reasonable. But more aggressive activities that reduce diversification or involve a subsidy are inappropriate.

Conclusion

This chapter has addressed the efficacy of social investing and the desirability of public and private pension funds engaging in such activity. In the end, one's view of efficacy depends on one's assessment of the efficiency of capital markets. If capital markets are efficient and the demand for a firm's stock is virtually elastic, screening is unlikely to have any impact on the company's cost of capital or the price of its stock. If the stock price dips temporarily below the level consistent with the discounted value of future earnings, investors not involved with screening will swoop in, buy shares, and restore the price. Similarly, in terms of community or economically targeted investments, in the face of efficient capital markets investors are unlikely to turn up investments that yield market returns and accomplish other goals. Finally, shareholder advocacy may create headlines, but it appears to have little measurable impact on the company's performance. Thus, with efficient capital markets, social investing probably has no real impact on the economy.

In terms of desirability, social investing seems appropriate only when the interests of the decision makers and the stakeholders are aligned. Certainly that is not the case with public pensions. Moreover, it is dangerous in a politically charged environment to permit decision makers to deviate from the pursuit of maximum return for a given level of risk. Public plans have gotten into trouble in the past when they have added social considerations to their list of criteria for selecting investments. In the case of private plans, where the stakeholders' and decision makers' interests are more likely to be aligned, screening is probably a relatively costless way for participants to make a statement. But these plans should not engage in activities that sacrifice returns for social goals; the pension fund is not an appropriate mechanism for gift-giving.

Fortunately, in recent years remarkably little social investing has taken place at the state and local level. This is an encouraging sign when considering equity investment for Social Security—either in the form of broadening trust-fund options or introducing personal accounts. Moreover, public plans lack the protections envisioned for Social Security. Little attempt is made to keep politicians away from public plans; in fact, many plans have the state treasurer or other elected officials sitting on the pension board.

Certainly those who advocate investing the Social Security trust funds in equities have proposed structures that would keep politics out of the process. Most suggest that Congress establish an expert investment board, very similar to the Federal Reserve Board, or to the Federal Retirement Thrift Investment Board that administers the Thrift Savings Plan for federal employees. To insulate this board from political influence, members would be appointed for long and staggered terms. The board would select a broad index fund, such as the Russell 3000 or the Wilshire 5000, and hire, on a competitive basis, private-sector pension managers to manage this portfolio.

Such an arrangement differs sharply from many state and local plans, which are still run in-house and involve the selection of individual stocks. The safeguards envisioned for equity investment in the trust funds should prevent even the modest amount of social investing that occurs at the state and local level. Comparable provisions could be designed for equity investment through personal Social Security accounts. The primary goal of investing retirement funds—through employer-sponsored pensions, union plans, state and local pensions, or Social Security—should be achieving the maximum returns for a given level of risk.

Notes

1. Social Investment Forum, *2003 Report on Socially Responsible Investing Trends in the United States* (Washington, D.C.: SIF Industry Research Program, 2003), available at http://www.ici.org/stats/latest/trends_12_03.html#TopOfPage (accessed May 17, 2005).

2. The largest funds omitted from table 1 are as follows: (1) The Boilermakers' Co-Generation and Infrastructure Fund: Project Finance ($6.8 billion), which co-invests in the construction of power generation plants that are then leased or sold to independent power producers, industrial companies, or the government. The Boilermakers & Blacksmiths National Pension Trust is the sole investor in the fund. (2) The Longview Collective Investment Fund ($5.4 billion), which is sponsored by the Amalgamated Bank, an institution that provides trust, investment advisory, custodial, and benefits remittance services for Taft-Hartley and public-sector employee benefit plans. (3) The Multi-Employer Property Trust Fund, an open-end equity real estate fund comprised of 241 multi-employer and public-employee pension plans that invests in high-quality, income-producing office buildings, warehouses, flex/R&D facilities, retail centers, hotels, and apartments. (4) The AFL-CIO Housing Investment Trust Fund ($3.4 billion), a pooled pension fund that invests in affordable housing developments throughout the United States. Social Investment Forum, *2003 Report on Socially Responsible Investing Trends*.

3. Washington Investors Mutual Fund, Inc, "Statement of Additional Information," *2004 Prospectus* (Washington, D.C.: American Funds, 2004), available at http://www.americanfunds.com/pdf/mfgepb-901_wmifb.pdf (accessed May 17, 2005).

4. U.S. Board of Governors of the Federal Reserve, *Flow of Funds Accounts* (Washington, D.C.: Federal Reserve Board, 2004). This reports that mutual fund assets, excluding money-market mutual funds, totaled $4.9 trillion in the fourth quarter of 2003.

5. Alisa Gravitz from the Social Investment Forum maintains that the reporting error for the Boilermakers' investments is simply one of labeling—claiming that, in fact, the entire Boilermakers' National Trust Fund is socially invested. However, conversations with Mario Rodriguez, the chief investment officer of the Boilermakers' pension funds, contradict the SIF claim. According to Rodriguez, "The SIF info is incorrect." Information obtained from phone interviews with Ms. Gravitz and Mr. Rodriguez.

6. Social Investment Forum, *2003 Report on Socially Responsible Investing Trends in the United States.*

7. SSGA has socially screened portfolios in nearly every asset class, including passive and active funds, U.S. and non-U.S. portfolios, small-cap equity, fixed-income, and cash portfolios. Although most of this money is screened for tobacco, SSGA has many accounts with a wider variety of screens. One actively managed fund has about $300 million screens for a broad array of social concerns, including alcohol, tobacco, gaming, and weapons. It also has an environmental and human rights screen, and separate proxy voting.

8. Interview with the Boston College Office of the Financial Vice President and Treasurer, conducted May 2004.

9. Social Investment Forum, *2003 Report on Socially Responsible Investing Trends in the United States.*

10. Ibid., 3.

11. S. Grossman and J. E. Stiglitz, "On the Impossibility of Informationally Efficient Markets," *American Economic Review* 70, no. 3 (1980): 393–408; A. S. Kyle, "Continuous Auctions and Insider Trading," *Econometrica* 53, no. 6 (1985): 1315–35.

12. Myron S. Scholes, "The Market for Securities: Substitution versus Price Pressure and the Effects of Information on Share Prices," *Journal of Business* 45, no. 2 (April 1972); R. W. Holthausen and Mayers D. Leftwich, "The Effect of Large Block Transactions on Security Prices. A Cross-Sectional Analysis," *Journal of Financial Economics* 19, no. 2 (1987): 237–67, looked at large block trades; and Claudio Loderer, John W. Cooney, and Leonard D. van Drunen, "The Price Elasticity of Demand for Common Stock," *Journal of Finance* 46 (1991): 109–26, examined seasoned equity offerings. Except for the early study by Scholes, these papers typically found price effects, but it was not easy for them to control for the information conveyed by the event.

13. Andrei Shleifer, "Do Demand Curves for Stocks Slope Down?" *Journal of Finance* 41, no. 3 (1986): 579–90.

14. A. Lynch and R. Mendenhall, "New Evidence on Stock Price Effects Associated with Changes in the S&P 500 Index," *Journal of Business* 70, no. 3 (1997): 351–83; R. Morck and F. Yang, "The Mysterious Growing Value of S&P 500 Membership," National Bureau of Economic Research working paper, 2001, http://papers.nber.org/papers/w8654.pdf (accessed May 17, 2005).

15. This discussion comes from Antti Petajisto, "What Makes Demand Curves for Stocks Slope Down?" Yale School of Management working paper,

November 15, 2003, http://icf.som.yale.edu/pdf/dcurve54.pdf (accessed May 17, 2005).

16. Robert C. Merton, "A Simple Model of Capital Market Equilibrium with Incomplete Information," *Journal of Finance* 42, no. 3 (1987): 483–510.

17. Merton, "A Simple Model," clearly states that the effect of his analyses is "likely to be most important for smaller and lesser-known firms," 487.

18. James J. Angel and Pietra Rivoli, "Does Ethical Investing Impose a Cost Upon the Firm? Theoretical Examination," *Journal of Investing* 6, no. 4 (1997): 57–61.

19. Siew Hong Teoh, Ivo Welch, and C. Paul Wazzan, "The Effect of Socially Activist Investment Policies on the Financial Markets: Evidence from the South Africa Boycott," *Journal of Business* 72, no. 1 (1999): 35–89.

20. During the 1970s, as opposition against the apartheid government increased, social activists charged that companies investing in South Africa indirectly supported the government and its discrimination policies. In an initial effort to resolve the conflict, the Reverend Leon Sullivan in 1977 introduced a set of guidelines for companies doing business in South Africa, the so-called Sullivan principles. By 1987, 127 U.S. companies had signed onto the Sullivan principles. Stuart Auerbach, "Sullivan Abandons S. African Conditions: Activist Minister Urges U.S. Firms to Leave Country," *Washington Post*, June 4, 1987, E1.

21. All the portfolios being invested in the most efficient manner possible involve some risk, and investors may also want to include some risk-free investment, such as treasury bills, in their portfolios.

22. Richard A. Brealey and Stewart C. Myers, *Principles of Corporate Finance* (New York: McGraw-Hill Education, 1996).

23. Burton Malkiel, "Socially Responsible Investing," speech to 1971 endowment conference, reprinted in *Classics II: Another Investor's Anthology*, ed. Charles Ellis (Homewood, Ill.: AIMR/BusinessOne Irwin, 1991).

24. Blake R. Grossman and William Sharpe, "Financial Implications of South African Divestment," *Financial Analysts Journal* 42, no. 4 (1986): 15–29.

25. Roberta Romano, "Pension Fund Activism in Corporate Governance Reconsidered," *Columbia Law Review* 93, no. 4 (1993): 795–853.

26. Alicia H. Munnell and Annika Sundén, "Investment Practices of State and Local Pension Plans," in *Pensions in the Public Sector*, ed. Olivia Mitchell and Edwin C. Hustead (Philadelphia: Pension Research Council and University of Pennsylvania Press, 2001).

27. John B. Guerard, "Is There a Cost to Being Socially Responsible in Investing?" *Journal of Investing* 6, no. 2 (1997): 11–19; S. Hamilton, H. Jo, and M. Statman, "Doing Well While Doing Good? The Investment Performance of Socially Responsible Mutual Funds," *Financial Analysts Journal* 49, no. 6 (1993): 62–66; M. Statman, "Socially Responsible Mutual Funds," *Financial Analysts Journal* (May 2000): 30–38; Bob Bauer, Kees Koedijk, and Roger Otten, "International Evidence on Ethical Fund Performance and Investment Style," University of Maastricht working paper, June 2002; Phoebus J. Dhrymes, "Socially Responsible Investment: Is It Profitable?" in *The Investment Research Guide to Socially Responsible Investing*, ed. Brian R. Bruce, Colloquium on Socially Responsible Investing, 1998; and Bernell K. Stone, John B. Guerard Jr., Mustafa N. Gultekin, and Greg Adams, "Socially Responsible Investment Screening: Strong Evidence of No Significant Cost for Actively Managed Portfolios," *Journal of Investing* (forthcoming).

A similar result has been found for bond portfolios. Louis D'Antonio, Tommie Johnsen, and R. Bruce Hutton, "Expanding Socially Screened Portfolios: An Attribution Analysis of Bond Performance," *Journal of Investing* 6, no. 4 (1997): 79–86.

28. Dan DiBartolomeo, "A View of Tobacco Divestiture by CalSTRS," Northfield Information Services, working paper, April 2000. In the late 1980s and early 1990s tobacco stocks performed slightly better than the S&P 500, but during the second half of the 1990s the tobacco stocks underperformed the S&P 500 on a risk-adjusted basis. Social Investment Forum, "Tobacco's Changing Context," in *1999 Tobacco Report* (Washington, D.C.: Social Investment Forum, 1999); Mark Ferrari, "Historical Risk and Return of the Tobacco Industry," in *Tobacco Divestment and Fiduciary Responsibility: A Legal and Financial Analysis*, ed. Douglas G. Cogan (Washington, D.C.: Investor Responsibility Research Center, 2000). However, the overall effect of divesting tobacco stocks should be small, because tobacco stocks only account for about 1 percent of the S&P 500.

29. Lawrence Kurtz and Dan DiBartolomeo, "Socially Screened Portfolios: An Attribution Analysis of Relative Performance," *Journal of Investing* 5 (Autumn 1996): 35–41; Dan DiBartolomeo and Lawrence Kurtz, "Explaining and Controlling the Returns of Socially Screened Portfolios," Northfield Information Services working paper, 1999, http://www.northin fo.com/papers/pdf/19990909_social_screen.pdf (accessed May 17, 2005).

30. M. Statman, "Socially Responsible Mutual Funds," *Financial Analysts Journal* (May 2000): 30–38; Christopher Luck and Nancy Pilotte, "Domini Social Index Performance," *Journal of Investing* (Fall 1993): 60–62.

31. These models state that portfolios are good substitutes if their exposure to the "factors" is equivalent and the portfolios are large enough to diversify away idiosyncratic risk.

32. Christopher C. Geczy, Robert F. Stambaugh, and David Levin, "Investing in Socially Responsible Mutual Funds," Wharton School working paper, 2003, http://finance.wharton.upenn.edu/~geczy/Papers/GSL_sri_paper_5_26_2003.pdf (accessed May 17, 2005).

33. Hewson Baltzell, "Refuting Media Bias against SRI," *Business Ethics* 17, no. 4 (2003), http://www.business-ethics.com/why_the_new_york_times_got_it_wrong.htm (accessed May 17, 2005).

34. Moskowitz was one of the first to suggest that a screened portfolio might outperform an unscreened portfolio, in Milton Moskowitz, "Choosing Socially Responsible Stocks," *Business and Society*, no. 1 (1972): 71–75.

35. Michael V. Russo and Paul A. Fouts, "A Resource-Based Perspective on Corporate Environmental Performance and Profitability," *Academy of Management Journal* 40, no. 3 (1997): 534–59. Other studies that have found positive effects of firms with good environmental policies include Mark Cohen, Scott A. Fenn, and Shameek Konar, "Environmental and Financial Performance: Are They Related?" Investor Responsibility Research Center working paper, Vanderbilt University, Nashville (May 1997), http://www.vanderbilt.edu/vcems/papers/irrc.pdf (accessed May 17, 2005); and Herbert D. Blank and C. Michael Carty, "The Eco-Efficiency Anomaly," Innovest working paper, June 2002, http://www.innovestgroup.com/pdfs/Eco_Anomaly_7_02.pdf (accessed May 17, 2005).

36. Stanley Feldman, Peter Soyka, and Paul Ameer, "Does Improving a Firm's Environmental Management System and Environmental Performance Result in a Higher Stock Price?" *Journal of Investing* 6, no. 4 (1997): 87–97.

37. Sandra A. Waddock and Samuel B. Graves, "Finding the Link between Stakeholder Relations and Quality of Management," *Journal of Investing* 6, no. 4 (1997): 20–24; Waddock and Graves, "Assessing the Link between Corporate Governance and Social/Financial Performance," International Association for Business and Society, 1999 proceedings (forthcoming).

38. For example, Lloyd Kurtz and Chris Luck, "An Attribution Analysis of the 100 Best Companies to Work for in America," presentation to Northfield Investment Conference, Fish Camp, California, May 5–7, 2002.

39. Social Investment Forum, *2003 Report on Socially Responsible Investing Trends*, 45.

40. Catherine Hickey, "Extending the Socially Responsible Investor," *Morningstar*, June 30, 2000.

41. Mary Williams Walsh, "Concerns Raised over Consultants to Pension Funds," *New York Times*, March 21, 2004, 1.

42. Jennifer Harris, *2001 Survey of State and Local Government Retirement Systems: Survey Report for Members of the Public Pension Coordinating Council* (Chicago: Public Retirement Institute, 2002).

43. *Employee Retirement Income Security Act, U.S. Code*, vol. 29, sec. 1104 (2000).

44. Mary Williams Walsh, "Political Money Said to Sway Pension Investments," *New York Times*, February 10, 2004, 1.

45. Furthermore, views on social investing are likely to differ within the group of stakeholders; Alan Neal, "Pension Funds and Socially Responsible Investment," East London School of Business working paper, Summer 2001.

46. Two books were instrumental to broadening the social investing debate: Jeremy Rifkin and Randy Barber, *The North Will Rise Again: Pensions, Politics and Power in the 1980s* (Boston: Beacon Press, 1978); and Lawrence Litvak, *Pension Funds and Economic Renewal* (Washington, D.C.: Council of State Planning Agencies, 1981).

47. Alicia H. Munnell, "The Pitfalls of Social Investing: The Case of Public Pensions and Housing," *New England Economic Review* (September/October 1983): 20–40.

48. Litvak, *Pension Funds and Economic Renewal*, 1981.

49. Munnell and Sundén, "Investment Practices of State and Local Pension Plans."

50. Perhaps the most comprehensive listing of economically targeted investment (ETI) activity was by the Boice Dunham Group, which was commissioned by Goldman Sachs to explore whether the growth in ETI activity might have created a market for Goldman Sachs services. An ETI was defined as "an investment by a public pension fund which, in addition to offering financial returns in proportion to financial risk, also offers collateral local economic benefit (e.g., job creation, home ownership)." Using this definition, Boice Dunham concluded that ETIs accounted for $17.5 billion, or 2 percent, of the $887.3 billion of assets covered by their survey—roughly 73 percent of total state and local assets. Boice Dunham Group, "The Nature and Scale of Economically-Targeted Investments by the Largest U.S. Public Pension Plans," report prepared for Goldman Sachs, 1993.

The second source of information on ETI activity comes from the U.S. Government Accounting Office, "Federal Research: Interim Report on the

Small Business Innovation Research Program," RCED-95-99 (March 8, 1995). Out of the 119 respondents to a survey, 50 indicated that they had invested a total of $19.8 billion in ETIs to promote housing, real estate, or small business development. This amounted to 2.4 percent of total respondents' assets. Since the respondents accounted for 85 percent of the assets of state and local plans, the results were broadly representative. At the low end in terms of identifying investments as ETIs were the Surveys of State and Local Employee Retirement Systems for Members of the Public Pension Coordinating Council in Paul Zorn, "Survey of State and Local Government Employee Retirement Systems," Survey Report for the Members of the Public Pension Coordinating Council, 1991, 1993, 1995, 1997. The question included in these surveys varied slightly over time, but generally asked, "What percentage of the portfolio is directed in-state for developmental purposes?" The emphasis on "developmental purposes" could easily have led respondents to omit residential mortgages made at market rates and private placements—the two largest categories in the Boice Dunham study. As a result, the proportion of total assets designated for in-state investment averaged between 0.1 percent and 0.3 percent over the four surveys.

51. Investor Responsibility Research Center, *Corporate Governance Bulletin* (Washington, D.C.: 1998).

52. Peter G. Pan and Jean Kadooka Mardfin, "Socially Responsible Investing," report no. 6 (Honolulu, Hawaii: Legislative Reference Bureau, 2001).

53. Walsh, "Concerns Raised over Consultants to Pension Funds."

54. Arleen Jacobius, "Disclosure Exemption," *Pensions and Investments*, April 5, 2004, 1.

55. Illinois Public Acts, no. 92-8064.

56. Walsh, "Concerns Raised," 1.

57. Alicia H. Munnell and Annika Sundén, *Coming Up Short: The Challenge of 401(k) Plans* (Washington, D.C.: Brookings Institution Press, 2004).

58. Michael Calabrese, "Building on Success: Labor-Friendly Investment Vehicles and the Power of Private Equity," in *Working Capital: The Power of Labor's Pensions*, ed. Archon Fung, Tessa Hebb, and Joel Rogers (Ithaca, N.Y.: Cornell University Press, 2001), 93–127.

59. Ibid.

60. Ibid.

61. Ibid.

62. Harry M. Markowitz, "Foundations of Portfolio Theory," *Journal of Finance* 46, no. 2 (1991): 469–77.

63. To the extent that these loans are non-recourse to the borrower or made to single-asset borrowers or are deeply subordinated or involve unproven technologies, the union may be taking on significant risk.

3

Why Social Investing Threatens Public Pension Funds, Charitable Trusts, and the Social Security Trust Fund

Charles E. Rounds Jr.

Introduction

Social investing is a precarious investment philosophy that cannot help but reflect the personal, financial, social, and/or political predilections of the investor. Human nature being what it is, trustees will be tempted to practice social investing, which can undermine their fiduciary duty of undivided loyalty to beneficiaries. Rarely, however, does a private trustee of a noncharitable personal trust, such as one that a parent in the estate-planning context might establish for his children, succumb to the temptation. Why do people in the private sector tend to behave differently from those in the public sector when it comes to the administration of other people's money?

There are two reasons. First, the private trustee would be subject to suit in state court by the beneficiaries for breach of duty of undivided loyalty, and any liability would be personal to the trustee.[1] Moreover, internal fiduciary liability insurance for private trustees can be prohibitively expensive.[2] Often it cannot be obtained at all.

Second, the public sector is not involved in the administration of the private noncharitable trust, other than as judicial arbiter of the rights, duties, and obligations of the parties. In other words, there are multiple legal safeguards in place to check a private trustee's impulses to practice social investing. The beneficiaries serve as independent private watchdogs of the activities of the private trustee, and the state court ensures that these watchdogs have nice, sharp teeth.[3]

When the government gets involved in the actual administration of a trust, however, legal checks and balances melt away, and the judicial watchdog loses its teeth. This is inevitable when the "state" becomes a party to a legal relationship, as well as its regulator and adjudicator. Take the California Public Employees' Retirement System (CalPERS), whose board is under fire for conflicts of interest so brazen that if it "were held to the same standards it demands of corporate America, . . . [it] . . . might have to fire itself."[4] Marbled throughout its enabling legislation are checks and balances that look good on paper, but legally are worthless. These paper safeguards regulating social investing include statutory self-dealing proscriptions; adoption of a prudent-investor rule similar to that found in the Employee Retirement Income Security Act (ERISA), the rigorous federal legislation governing the administration of private pension plans; and the establishment of a trust fund.[5]

As the California experience shows, when the government gets into the investment business, social investing and political patronage go hand-in-glove, and there is nothing much the law can do about it. A recent article in *Forbes* magazine had the provocative title "Sanctimonious in Sacramento: California public pension fund is making a big stink about little problems in the governance of companies these days . . . What about the stench from its own self-dealing?" It makes just that point:

> The theory behind CalPERS' attack on corporate boards is that directors should focus solely on maximizing returns. Yet CalPERS has invested billions in "economically targeted investments" aimed at providing "collateral benefits to targeted geographic areas, groups of people or sectors while providing pension funds with prudent investment." If such investments fall short, of course, California taxpayers can be forced to pick up the tab.[6]

The "state" is deeply involved in the administration of charitable funds as well. As a consequence, legal safeguards to prevent breaches of fiduciary duty, such as social investing, are for all intents and purposes as illusory in the charitable sector as they are in the public sector. With a few exceptions, enforcement responsibility falls to a state's attorney general—a politician—to oversee the administration of charitable funds.[7] In many states neither the donor of the funds nor the prospective recipients of the donor's largesse would have standing to bring an action in state or federal court to enjoin the trustees of the charitable trust, or the directors of the charitable corporation as the case may be, from engaging in social investing.[8] Only the state attorney general may bring the action; and if the attorney general is somehow complicit, then he may with impunity exercise an inherent discretionary authority not to do so. At this point, the public's only recourse is to interest the press in the matter, which is time-consuming and often futile, or wait until election day, an even less practical option.

The recent controversy over the Hershey charitable trust is an example of a state attorney general actually promoting social investing. In 1909, chocolate industrialist Milton S. Hershey and his wife, Catherine S. Hershey, created and endowed the Milton Hershey School.[9] The trust is currently worth approximately $10 billion, with approximately 50 percent of the trust portfolio in Hershey stock. The Pennsylvania attorney general sent signals to the board of trustees, which controlled 76 percent of the voting stock of the Hershey Foods Company, that it ought to consider prudently diversifying the portfolio of the charitable trust. In response, the board put the company on the auction block.

In September 2002, in the face of intense public outcry by the local Hershey, Pennsylvania, community, the board took the company off the auction block because the attorney general, who had set the whole process in motion, yielded to the public pressure and reversed his position. His reversal essentially forced the private fiduciaries to engage in social investing against their better judgment. This unfortunate series of events reinforces the old adage: "[R]etaining investments is in effect making them."[10]

Finally, in the context of the Social Security privatization debate, there have been calls for the federal government to invest FICA payments in the private sector:

> Proponents of Social Security privatization, including members of the president's commission on Social Security reform, have introduced a new argument for dramatically restructuring the system. They claim that the assets contained in the Social Security trust fund are not "real" but merely IOUs from the government. The assertion is wrong—and would be obviously so if Social Security were able to acquire corporate equities and bonds in the same way that private pension funds, public employee pension funds and the Canada Pension Plan (the Canadian equivalent of Social Security) do.[11]

First, the Social Security bonds that are ostensibly in the so-called Social Security trust fund are neither legally "real" nor are they enforceable IOUs.[12] As a matter of law, neither they nor the trust fund exist. (As President Bill Clinton explained in his fiscal 2000 budget, these trust fund balances "do not consist of real economic assets that can be drawn down in the future to fund benefits. Instead they are claims on the Treasury that, when redeemed, will have to be financed by raising taxes, borrowing from the public, or reducing benefits or other expenditures."[13]) Second, if social investing is rampant in CalPERS, whose enabling legislation is laden with paper checks and balances and nice-sounding fiduciary language, then as surely as water flows downhill, it would be rampant if the federal government through its agents were to get into the business of investing FICA receipts.

In this chapter I explain why it is that in the United States, when the "state," as that term is employed generically, gets into the business of administering or supervising the administration of other people's money, any legal safeguards designed to deter improper social investing are not worth the paper they are printed on. They are, in lawyers' parlance, illusory. The problem cannot legally be corrected unless there are fundamental structural reforms that remove the "state" from the equation. What about the European experience with money management by public entities, which some have suggested has been a salutary one? Because the legal and political traditions of continental Europe and the United States are so different—in most European jurisdictions, for example, the trust is not even recognized[14]—the European experience can inform the United States social investing debate only at the margins.[15]

Unless public pension funds are entrusted to an independent private trustee, for example a bank or trust company, such that the entity assumes the actual legal title, "explicit organizational mandates to maximize return on contributors' investment," "independent boards of trustees," and "contracting out portfolio management on a competitive basis" are safeguards in form only.[16] There is no legal substance to them, as the CalPERS experience so amply demonstrates.

In the case of a fund for charitable purposes, there are some things a prospective benefactor and his lawyer can do at the document-drafting stage to deter the fiduciaries, be they directors of a charitable corporation or trustees, from engaging in social investing. They can put provisions into the governing corporate or trust documentation, the effect of which is to privatize oversight of the fund's administration substantially. Once the gift is completed, however, it is usually too late to tweak the documentation. A benefactor who discovers that a fiduciary has been socially investing his entrusted charitable gift would have little recourse other than to jawbone the press—or to make another contribution, this time to the attorney general's political war chest.

With respect to the investment of Social Security tax receipts, if one is concerned that there be a modicum of legal accountability for social investing, then entrusting the federal government and/or its agents with the responsibility of investing the receipts in corporate equities and bonds is not the way to go. In fact, it would be asking for real trouble; CalPERS meet Hershey. One who proposes that the federal government get into the investment business appreciates neither the limits of the law nor the fallibility of human nature.

If meaningful fiduciary accountability for social investing is a desirable societal goal, then Social Security privatization is the only option that brings with it legal safeguards with teeth. FICA payments must be segregated. Either private trustees who are amenable to the law or the taxpayers themselves must take legal title to the property. There is precedent for the latter in the Individual Retirement Account (IRA) context. And, finally, unlike the present Social Security welfare scheme, the taxpayers must have ownership rights in the property.[17] Without these reforms, social investing is an inevitable byproduct of the government getting into the investment business. It comes with the territory.

The concept that the "state" for all intent and purposes is legally unaccountable is not a new one. As far back as 1830, Justice Putnam, in the landmark Massachusetts trust case *Harvard College v. Amory*, raised concerns about governmental accountability in the context of investment selection:

> There is one consideration much in favor of . . . [private trustees] . . . investing in the stock of private corporations. They are amenable to the law. The holder may pursue his legal remedy and compel them or their officers to do justice. But the government can only be supplicated.[18]

Trustees and Social Investment

A trust is a tangle of legal and equitable relationships with respect to property.[19] Although the trustee has legal title to the property, it is segregated from his own. It is the beneficiary who has the equitable or economic interest in the property, not the trustee. The trustee is a fiduciary, which means that the trustee owes to the beneficiary certain duties, such as the duty not to self-deal with the trust property and the duty not to commingle trust property with the trustee's own property.[20] If the trustee breaches a fiduciary duty to the beneficiary, the beneficiary may seek redress in the courts.[21] A trustee who self-deals in breach of his trust, for example, breaches his general duty of undivided loyalty to the beneficiary, which is the duty to act solely in the interest of the beneficiary.[22]

A trustee who socially invests trust property seeks to use the investment process "to promote nonfinancial social goals."[23] That is the lawyer's definition. Whether in any given situation a particular social investment in some way undermines the beneficiary's equitable or economic interest is legally irrelevant. What is legally relevant is that the loyalties of the trustee are divided. For good or for ill, the trustee is not acting "solely in the interest of the beneficiary."[24] Even if it is economically feasible for a trustee without "sacrificing returns" to indulge his, her, or its own social and political predilections with other people's money, even if for every politically incorrect investment there is an economically comparable, politically correct, economically targeted investment (ETI), we are still haunted by Justice Cardozo's admonition against the adoption of "particular exceptions" to a fiduciary's duty of undivided loyalty:

> A trustee is held to something stricter than the morals of the marketplace. Not honesty alone, but the punctilio of an honor the most sensitive, is then the standard of behavior. As to this there has developed a tradition that is unbending and inveterate. Uncompromising rigidity has been the attitude of courts of equity when petitioned to undermine the rule of undivided loyalty by the "disintegrating erosion" of particular exceptions.[25]

Moreover, even though a pension or charitable trust may occasionally emerge economically unscathed from a trustee's foray into the realm of social investing, there are still the overarching societal implications of having vast concentrations of economic wealth, and the political power that goes with it, in the hands of a relatively few fiduciaries with social and political agendas.

For those who are skeptical of social investing, the question then becomes, is there is anything that *legally* can be done to deter a trustee altogether from socially investing either public pension or charitable trust funds? Or, if social investing is inevitable, can the trustee be legally deterred from sacrificing returns in the pursuit of personal and political goals? Without an answer to this threshold question, one cannot have a rational debate about how to reform Social Security, how to depoliticize state pension programs, or how to shore up the principle of donor intent when it comes to the investment of endowment funds or funds held in charitable trusts and corporations.

For the most part, legal safeguards intended to prevent the states from socially investing pension funds, private fiduciaries from socially investing charitable funds, and the United States from socially investing the phantom Social Security trust fund are, or would be, illusory without major structural reforms that have the effect of taking the "state" out of the investment game. Under the auspices of its judiciary, the "state" should merely act as a referee, and it should do so from the sidelines. In the case of CalPERS and other state-run pension funds, safeguards in the absence of structural reform are illusory because title to the trust funds remains in the "state" or its instrumentalities.[26] In the case of charitable funds, it is because the state attorney general, a politician, is charged by law with primary, and often exclusive, oversight responsibility. In the case of Social Security as it is currently structured, it is because the government, and not the taxpayers, owns the FICA tax payments.[27]

State Pension Funds

The debate among the politicians, economists, and opinion makers over whether the United States should be authorized to invest FICA tax payments in private equities and/or public and private debt often seems divorced from constitutional and legal reality. Supporters and opponents of a portion of the so-called Social Security trust fund in equities, for example, have suggested there are lessons to be learned from an examination of the social investment practices of state governments.[28] Those who advocate partial privatization suggest there has been rampant social investing at the state and local levels:[29]

Yucaipa's managing partner, Ronald W. Burkle, is a billionaire and has been a substantial donor to many politicians, including Mr. Clinton and several past and present trustees of CalPERS. In 2001, CalPERS voted to commit $450 million to three Yucaipa private investment funds, which were designed to generate returns and societal benefits, by financing neglected businesses in poor neighborhoods and companies that treat workers conscientiously. CalPERS' most recent annual report showed that these funds have drawn about $51 million in total investments and related fees, and have so far not produced returns.[30]

Opponents of privatization question how much actual social investing has actually been going on:[31]

> The latest effort to promote government investment . . . [of Social Security funds] . . . is an op-ed in the *Washington Post* by Alicia Munnell and R. Kent Weaver. . . . [T]hey propose that the Social Security trust fund be allowed to invest in "corporate equities and bonds in the same way that private pension funds, public employee pension funds and the Canada Pension Plan do." Doing so, they argue, "offers the advantage of individual accounts without the risk and costs."[32]

As a preliminary matter, it needs to be pointed out that in many respects each side is comparing entities that legally are apples and oranges. The United States and the State of California are neither legally nor constitutionally comparable. Unlike Congress when it "created" the phantom Social Security trust fund, the California legislature created CalPERS "solely for the benefit of the members and retired members of . . . [the] . . . system and their survivors and beneficiaries."[33] Moreover, by law the pension rights of a California public employee "may not be destroyed, once vested, without impairing a contractual obligation of the employing public entity."[34]

Unlike a participant in Social Security, which is legally a welfare program that creates no private property rights,[35] a California public employee would have a property right in his accrued pension benefits that would warrant the protections of the takings clause of the Fifth Amendment to the U.S. Constitution, article 1, section 10, clause 1 of the Constitution having prohibited a state from passing a law impairing the obligations of contracts. Moreover, unlike the Social Security welfare recipient,[36] he would have standing to seek redress in the courts should California interfere with those contractual property rights.[37]

Accordingly, when it comes to the social investment of assets in the CalPERS fund, the worker, a private citizen, in theory would have standing to go into court and seek to enjoin the CalPERS board from continuing to abuse its trust. His or her counsel would argue that "the interest of the employee at issue is in the security and integrity of the funds to pay future benefits."[38] Moreover, the California cases suggest that a CalPERS beneficiary would also have a cause of action against the state were the board's social investment practices actually to interfere with his or her defined benefit. In other words, the beneficiary could sue the State of California for breach of contract. But the victory could well be a pyrrhic one:

> It does not necessarily follow . . . that the pensioner possesses the ability to compel the payment of benefits as they mature. If the Legislature fails to appropriate sums from the general fund for the purpose of funding the special retirement account or otherwise paying the state's indebtedness to pensioners, a court of this state is powerless to compel the Legislature to appropriate such sums or to order payment of the indebtedness.[39]

The problem with the government getting into the investment business is a practical one: It is hugely expensive and time consuming for a member of the public to take on the full might of the state in an action for breach of fiduciary duty. In California, the cards are particularly stacked against the petitioner. On June 5, 2003, for example, California's attorney general rendered a legal opinion that CalPERS may allow its fiduciaries to purchase "waivers of recourse" coverage from its own self-insurance program, thus effectively enabling them to engage in social investment with impunity.[40] Bottom line: When the government gets involved in investing the property of others, the law talks loudly but carries a very small stick.

Those charged with administering the CalPERS fund are politicians, political appointees, agents of politicians, and agents of political appointees.[41] The state attorney general, of course, is a politician as well. When politicians get into the business of investing other people's money, the temptation to use the attendant economic power for partisan political purposes is irresistible. It should come as no surprise that "many investments by the $166 billion . . . [CalPERS] fund have increasingly focused on satisfying the political goals of labor and the Democratic Party faithful."[42]

The situation is no better in New York. During the 2004 Bush-Kerry presidential election battle, New York State's Democratic comptroller, Alan Hevesi, wrote a letter in his capacity as trustee of the state pension fund to the Sinclair Broadcast Group, suggesting that if it aired the anti-Kerry film *Stolen Honor* it would risk alienating "regulators."[43] The fund held 265,000 shares in the company. The letter suggested that the airing of this particular film would erode shareholder value. Would the same letter have been issued had the film been *Fahrenheit 9/11*?

One also would be ill advised to count on a state's auditor general or treasurer to oversee public pension funds in an orderly, focused, and nonpartisan way. Both Democratic and Republican politicians may have political axes to grind. Take the matter of Pennsylvania's public school teachers' and state employees' funds, which have had investment losses in the neighborhood of $20 billion while incurring $250 million a year in management fees:

> This disaster spurred Pennsylvania's Auditor General Bob Casey to launch an investigation. And as the state's chief financial officer, he had every right to do so. But he was stymied by state Treasurer Barbara Hafer, a

Republican, who has spent the last year in an expensive legal battle to resist the Democrat's subpoenas. Mr. Casey, who is running to replace Ms. Hafer, wants to know the details of how the contracts to manage the funds are awarded.[44]

Mounting a citizens' campaign to interest the media in shining a spotlight on a public retirement board's social investing practices can be time consuming and marked only by fleeting, modest success, generally at the margins:

> Despite CalPERS' frequent calls for full disclosure by companies, it can be a little reticent itself. Two years ago the fund refused to release details on the returns racked up by its private equity investments, which total some $7.8 billion. The *San Jose Mercury* had to go to court to get hold of the data. CalPERS argued it wanted to disclose the data but was prevented by a confidentiality agreement with Grove Street Advisors, a firm it hired to assemble private equity funds. A judge disagreed. A year ago the *Mercury News* disclosed that one director, Angelides, had received political contributions from some Grove Street–related funds.[45]

Charitable Funds

Unlike a personal trust that a parent might establish for a child, it is in the nature of the typical charitable trust for the "beneficiaries" to be so numerous and their interests so contingent and tangential that, as a practical matter, no beneficiary possesses a sufficient interest to seek its enforcement in the courts. This applies as well to charitable corporations. While each of us, for example, is both a direct and indirect contingent beneficiary of endowed medical research, in essence it is all of us *collectively*—the *public*, as it were—who is the beneficiary. Thus, for hundreds of years both in the

United States and in England, the "duty of maintaining the rights of the public and of a number of persons too indefinite to vindicate their own has vested in the [state] and is exercised . . . through the [state] attorney general."[46] This is a practical solution to the enforceability dilemma inherent in the charitable trust and corporation. The alternative—vesting everyone with standing to seek judicial enforcement—would be intolerably chaotic and impractical. The downside, of course, is that, as already mentioned, the state attorney general is a politician.

To say, however, that a state attorney general "oversees" public charities is not to suggest that he or she "audits" them. Until relatively recently, most overworked and understaffed attorneys general had no idea even how many charitable trusts they were supposed to be "overseeing." Many a charitable trust was going unperformed for one reason or another, including indifference, neglect, or death of the trustee. In an effort to get an accurate running head count of how many charitable trusts are running or supposed to be running at any given time, and to maintain as well a depository of basic information regarding them, many states have enacted statutes requiring that charitable trustees and directors of charitable corporations make certain periodic filings with their respective attorneys general. In some states, the reporting and licensing function is handled by a separate agency altogether, such as the office of secretary of state or some consumer protection bureaucracy. In ten states, there is no general system of registration and reporting whatsoever.

These reforms have enhanced somewhat the oversight of charitable trusts, if only because these informational filings are generally available for public inspection. In other words, an element of privatization has been injected into the process. Still, most state attorneys general lack the staffing, resources, and organizations to oversee charities properly. Only eleven offices have designated sections staffed by three or more full-time attorneys. According to James Fishman, "Staffing problems and a relative lack of interest in monitoring nonprofits make attorney general oversight more theoretical than deterrent."[47]

What, if anything, can be done to rein in fiduciaries bent on socially investing charitable funds when the state attorney general is either occupied with other things or intentionally looking the other way? There is some case law to the effect that private persons having a special interest in the performance of a charitable trust can maintain a suit for its enforcement. However, they must show that their interest is not merely derived from their status as members of the general public. One may have standing if one is entitled to a preference under the terms of the trust, is a member of a small class of identifiable beneficiaries, or is certain to receive trust benefits. Thus, the holder of an endowed chair at a medical research facility would have standing to seek enforcement of the endowment trust. Rights to seek enforcement would also accrue to a minister entitled to income distributions from a clergy support trust. Some states (California, for example) by statute allow for some donor involvement in the fiduciary oversight process by granting a donor access to the courts to seek the removal of a trustee for breach of fiduciary duty—for example, the social investment of the trust property.[48]

In the absence of a statutory grant of standing, however, the donor of a charitable gift will have an uphill battle attempting to obtain it from a court. If standing is denied, the donor's only recourse is to importune the state attorney general to get involved. Most donors, however, do not have the requisite political clout to force a dilatory or reluctant attorney general to do the right thing. In one case, the Connecticut attorney general actually stood on the sidelines and watched a donor charity and a donee charity battle it out in the courts over whether the donor had standing to seek enforcement of certain grant restrictions that were allegedly being ignored by the donee.[49] The trial court determined that the Connecticut attorney general, not the donor charity, was vested with standing to seek enforcement of the restrictions in the courts. And with that, the case was thrown out of court. The actions of the trial court were upheld on appeal. Courts are even disinclined to grant institutional charitable donors standing to seek enforcement of charitable trusts.

Clearly, the default law of trusts and charitable corporations will not be particularly solicitous of any efforts on the part of a donor of a charitable gift to prevent the fiduciary, be it a trustee or a charitable corporation, from socially investing the donation. The benefactor, however, unlike the CalPERS beneficiary or the participant in the Social Security welfare scheme, may be able to take some prophylactic measures. A charitable donor may be able legally to privatize some of the fiduciary oversight responsibilities, provided he or she does so before the gift is made. While there are no guarantees, here are some countermeasures that the benefactor and counsel may want to consider taking in an effort to prevent the fiduciary from indulging his, her, or its social and political predilections with the donation:

- Establish the charitable trust in a state whose courts look at social investing with a jaundiced eye.

- Establish the charitable trust in a state whose Office of the Attorney General has a good track record of taking seriously its responsibility of overseeing charities and of reining in charitable fiduciaries who are practicing social investing without express authority to do so in the governing documentation.

- Avoid unrestricted gifts to charitable corporations.

- Avoid making a charity the trustee of a restricted gift for the benefit of the charity.

- Avoid making a governmental entity the trustee of a charitable gift.

- Put a sunset provision into the governing documentation, or provide that the donation shall be consumed within a reasonable period of time.

- Make sure that the charitable purposes are articulated with precision in the governing documentation, and include express prohibitions against social investing.

- Appoint more than one fiduciary to administer the donation, such as independent co-trustees.

- Draft the documentation in a way that bestows on the donor standing to seek enforcement of the trust in the courts.

- Draft the documentation in a way that bestows standing on persons other than the donor to seek enforcement of the fiduciary's charitable obligations so that the attorney general is not the only one with oversight responsibilities.

- Designate an independent, nongovernmental "trust protector" in the governing documentation.

Social Security

To engage in any discussion of social investing in the Social Security context, it is important to understand the legal principle, embedded in the U.S. Constitution, that *one Congress may not bind a future Congress*. When the United States issues a bond pursuant to the act of one Congress, it enters into a contract with the purchaser. In other words, the United States bestows property rights on the purchaser. While one's rights under a government bond may not be as "enforceable" as one's rights under a bond issued by a private entity, and therefore not as legally secure, they still constitute property. A future Congress legally could not take those rights away from the purchaser:

> Having this power to authorize the issue of definite obligations for the payments of money borrowed, the Congress has not been vested with authority to alter or destroy those obligations. The fact that the United States may not be sued without its consent is a matter of procedure which does not affect the legal and binding character of its contracts. While the Congress is under no duty to provide remedies through the courts, the contractual obligation still exists, and despite infirmities of procedure, remains binding upon the conscience of the sovereign.[50]

On the other hand, if one Congress establishes a welfare program, a future Congress could terminate that program with impunity. Why? Because no private property rights will have accrued.[51] There would be no one with standing to prevent the program's termination. Being a matter internal to the United States government, one Congress may not bind a future Congress.

As noted earlier, the current Social Security system, unlike CalPERS, is a welfare program that bestows no property rights on those who make FICA tax payments to the U.S. Treasury.[52] Moreover, the so-called Social Security bonds on file in some federal government office are mere accounting euphemisms.[53] A bond in the hands of its issuer is a nullity because one may not contract with oneself. Any Congress may repudiate these phantom instruments with impunity, and no citizen would have "standing" to seek redress in the courts. It is a matter internal to the government. Because the current Social Security system makes no enforceable promises or guarantees to the FICA taxpayer in exchange for the FICA tax payments, neither the Social Security statutes nor the U.S. Constitution afford the taxpayer any legal or constitutional safeguards. This is because under the current system, there is nothing to safeguard. Moreover, because the United States has in the past commingled and continues to commingle FICA tax payments with its general revenues, as is its legal right, it is nonsensical to accuse the United States of socially investing the FICA tax payments. True, it is spending the funds on purposes unrelated to Social Security. But spending is not investing.

If the United States were authorized under the Social Security system as it is currently structured to invest FICA tax payments in the private equity and debt markets, the FICA taxpayer would still be no better off. While the United States might acquire an ownership interest in a healthy chunk of corporate America, the FICA taxpayers themselves would not. For them, it would be status quo. That could not be said for corporate America, however.

The danger, of course, is that that power in the United States to take title to and vote massive blocks of stock could lead to rampant, hyperpoliticized social investing, that is to say, a form of backdoor socialism. While one Congress might attempt to put in place statutory safeguards against the politicization of the investment process—for example, by requiring that the United States shall have no power to vote the stock it invests in, or that investments be indexed, or that respected private-sector entities such as the Fidelity or Vanguard serve as investment agents of the United States—another Congress could easily dismantle these "safeguards," and the FICA taxpayers would be without recourse. Moreover, even if these paper "safeguards" were to remain on the statute books, the FICA taxpayer would have no standing to seek their enforcement in the courts in the event governmental entities charged with administering and overseeing the investment process chose to ignore them. Nor, likely, would an outraged member of Congress.[54]

In an era when the ends justify the means, when hyperpoliticized courts, attorneys general, and executive officers at all levels of government are with impunity picking and choosing what laws shall be enforced,[55] it would be naïve in the extreme to expect federal politicians and bureaucrats to refrain from inflicting their political and social predilections on corporate America if given half a chance, particularly if the United States and only the United States were the legal titleholder and the beneficial owner of the securities. The temptation would be too great.

Under the Social Security system as it is currently structured, there is no trust fund as that term is commonly understood. Because there is no trust fund, neither the United States nor any other entity is serving other than euphemistically as trustee. What if Congress were to require that going forward, the United States or an agent of the United States take title as trustee of a segregated fund of FICA payments and administer the funds for the benefit of the FICA taxpayers? There are two problems with this approach.

The first relates to another legal principle, this one embedded in Anglo-American common-law jurisprudence: One may not enforce a trust against the Crown without the Crown's permission. "At common law it was held that a use or trust could not be enforced against the Crown, since the sovereign could not be held liable in its own courts."[56] Today, one may transfer title to an item of property to the United States in trust for a particular purpose. The problem, however, is enforceability. Under the doctrine of sovereign immunity, those with the equitable or economic interest may not sue the United States without its consent.[57] Moreover, in cases where Congress has authorized suits against the United States for breach of trust, the record is clear that the United States has had an abysmal track record administering trusts. Take the case of the gross mismanagement by the United States of three hundred thousand trust fund accounts totaling $2.5 billion that had been established over a century ago for the benefit of certain Native Americans. In a *Wall Street Journal* editorial on the subject, Senator John McCain is quoted as saying that if anyone in the private sector had operated the way the government had, "they would be in jail today."[58] Implicit in his statement is that it will be a long time, if ever, before Indians recover a cent of the squandered funds. Bottom line: Even when a citizen ostensibly has been granted enforceable rights under a trust administered by the United States, those rights are for all intents and purposes illusory.[59]

It is highly unlikely that a Congress would grant every FICA taxpayer standing to litigate against the United States for breaches of trust of the common-law variety—for example, breaching the duty of loyalty by socially investing to the economic detriment of his or her equitable interest. It would simply be too chaotic.[60] And to bestow that right on the United States attorney general or some politically appointed watchdog group or commission is merely asking the fox to guard the henhouse.

The second problem is that under fundamental principles of trust law, a trustee takes the legal title to the trust property. To the world, the trustee is the owner of the property. From the perspective of corporate America, whether the United States is engaging in rampant social investing as trustee or as outright owner is a distinction without a difference. In either case, it is a form of backdoor socialism. The fact that the United States would be a trustee in name affords the private corporate sector little more than a paper safeguard against government abuse of the voting power.

Were Congress to allow a FICA taxpayer to retain some of what would otherwise be his or her FICA tax payments and to invest those funds privately in an IRA-type account, then there would be less of a risk of politics infecting the investment process than if the United States or its agents were to do the investing. This is because property rights would then accrue to the taxpayer, and title to that property would then be in the taxpayer. This corona of private ownership rights would substantially reduce the opportunity and temptation of government to engage in social investing and other such mischief-making, particularly as the takings clause of the Fifth Amendment would be implicated.[61] Thus, were the United States or any of its agents to attempt to violate those rights, the taxpayer would have standing to seek redress in the courts.[62]

But the constitutional safeguard of the takings clause would not be foolproof. The power of the United States to levy taxes would remain intact and virtually limitless.[63] As the United States could be expected to regulate heavily the privately administered commingled funds that would be on Social Security's menu of permissible investment vehicles, social investing could rear its ugly head in the regulatory context.[64] Still, possession—and certainly ownership—is nine-tenths of the law. Although under the current Social Security system all FICA payments are owned by the United States and therefore fair game for political exploitation, a politician is likely to think twice before indulging his or her social and political predilections with private property—that is, property that does not belong to the United States.

If the United States were to invest Social Security FICA tax payments either as the owner of the payments or as trustee in a segregated fund, any statutory safeguards put in place ostensibly to prevent the United States or its agents from engaging in socially investing funds would be illusory. This is because under either scenario, title to the payments would be in the United States or its agents. If title to the payments, on the other hand, were to remain with the FICA taxpayer, or be lodged in the *taxpayer's* agents, then the taxpayer would have the benefit of the constitutional and legal "safeguards" that come with private ownership.

Conclusion

There are many public-policy reasons for those charged with investing state pension funds, charitable funds, and the phantom Social Security trust fund to be prohibited from the practice of social investing. Social investing subverts a fiduciary's common-law duty of undivided loyalty. With respect to Social Security, the practice could serve as a vehicle for functionally nationalizing the United States economy. With respect to public pension funds, it serves as a vehicle for political mischief at the expense of the interests of taxpayers, not to mention those on the receiving end of the mischief. In the charitable context, it can undermine the institution of the trust, as well as the charitable inclinations of the citizenry. But merely outlining the public-policy case against social investing is not enough. We must offer legal solutions, as well; otherwise, we are just flailing in the air. Until an element of privatization is injected into the administration and oversight of these funds, any attempt by a legislature to rein in the social investors among us will be an exercise in futility.

Notes

1. See Charles Rounds Jr., *Loring: A Trustee's Handbook* (Frederick, Md.: Aspen Publishers, 2005), sec. 3.5.4.1 (discussing the personal liabilities of a private trustee).

2. Ibid., sec. 3.5.4.2 (discussing the limitations on a personal trustee's ability to insure against internal breaches of fiduciary duty).

3. Ibid., sec. 7.2.3 (discussing the panoply of equitable remedies available to a trust beneficiary if the trustee breaches his, her, or its fiduciary duties to the beneficiary).

4. Neil Weinberg, "Sanctimonious in Sacramento," *Forbes*, May 10, 2004, 52.

5. West's Ann.Cal.Gov.Code sec. 20150, 20151, and 20170.

6. Weinberg, "Sanctimonious in Sacramento."

7. See generally Rounds, *Loring*, sec. 9.4.2 (discussing who has standing to enforce charitable trusts).

8. Ibid.

9. See generally Rounds, *Loring*, sec. 8.35 (discussing the Hershey Trust).

10. *Dickerson v. Camden Trust Co.*, 140 N.J.Eq. 34, 42, 53 A.2d 225, 231 (1947).

11. Alicia H. Munnell and R. Kent Weaver, "How to Privatize Social Security," *Washington Post*, July 9, 2001, A19.

12. 42 USCA s 401(a); *Flemming v. Nestor*, 363 U.S. 603 (1960); *Helvering v. Davis*, 301 U.S. 619 (1937).

13. U.S Office of Management and Budget, *Budget of the United States Government, Fiscal Year 2000: Analytical Perspectives* (Washington, D.C.: U.S. Government Printing Office, 1999), 337. It should be emphasized that these phantom "claims" on the Treasury are unenforceable in the courts and may be repudiated by Congress.

14. See generally Rounds, *Loring*, sec. 8.12.1 (discussing civil law alternatives to the trust).

15. But see Munnell and Weaver, "How to Privatize Social Security," suggesting otherwise.

16. See generally ibid.

17. See *Helvering v. Davis*, in which the United States Supreme Court confirmed that Social Security as it is currently structured is a welfare program that creates no private rights.

18. *Harvard College v. Amory*, 26 Mass. (9 Pick) 446, 460 (1830).

19. An item of property is a collection of rights that are enforceable in some court by its owner. "The term 'property' denotes interests in things not the things themselves"; Restatement (Second) of Trusts sec. 2, cmt. c. If one owns or has a property interest in a bond, for example, one owns a collection of contractual rights that are enforceable in some court. These rights might include the right to be paid interest in the amounts and at the times specified in the governing instrument; the right to sell or give away the bond; and the right to keep third parties from seizing the bond. "Valid contracts are property, whether the obligor be a private individual, a municipality, a state, or the United States"; Lynch v. United States, 54 S.Ct. 840, 579 (1934).

20. Rounds, Loring, chapter 1; Rounds, sec. 3.5.1 (discussing nature and extent of the trustee's estate); Rounds, sec. 6.2.1.2 (discussing trustee's duty to segregate and earmark the trust property); Rounds, sec. 5.3.1 (discussing nature and extent of beneficiary's property interest).

21. Scott on Trusts, sec. 197.

22. Rounds, Loring, sec. 6.1.3 (discussing trustee's duty to be loyal to the trust).

23. John H. Langbein and Richard A. Posner, "Social Investing and the Law of Trusts," Michigan Law Review 79 (1980): 72, 73.

24. Uniform Trust Code, sec. 802(a); Restatement (Third) of Trusts, sec. 170(1) (1992); 2A Scott on Trusts, sec.170; Employee Retirement Income Security Act (ERISA), 29 U.S.C. sec. 1104(a)1, 404 (1974).

25. Meinhard v. Salmon, 249 N.Y. 458, 464, 164 N.E. 545, 546 (1928).

26. See, for example, West's Ann.Cal.Gov.Code, sec. 20170 (confirming that California's Public Employees' Retirement Fund is operated out of the state treasury), and sec. 20171 (providing that the California Board of Administration of the Public Employees' Retirement System has the exclusive control of the administration of the retirement fund).

27. Helvering v. Davis.

28. See generally Alicia H. Munnell and Annika Sundén, "Investment Practices of State and Local Pension Funds: Implications for Social Security Reform," prepared for presentation at the First Annual Joint Conference for the Retirement Consortium "New Developments in Retirement Research," May 20–21, 1999.

29. Ibid.

30. Mary Williams Walsh, "Concerns Raised Over Consultants to Pension Funds," New York Times, March 21, 2004.

31. See generally Munnell and Sundén, "Investment Practices of State and Local Pension Funds."

32. Michael Tanner, "Munnell Pushes Government Investing," Cato Institute Project on Social Security Choice, July 18, 2001, http://www.social security.org/daily/07-18-01.html (accessed May 17, 2005).

33. West's Ann.Cal.Gov.Code, sec. 20170.

34. *Valdes v. Cory*, 139 Cal.App.3d 773, 783–84, 189 Cal.Rptr. 212, 221 (1983).

35. *Helvering v. Davis.*

36. See *Flemming v. Nestor.*

37. See *Valdes v. Cory*, 189 Cal.Rptr. 212 (1983).

38. Ibid.

39. Ibid.

40. 86 Ops. Cal. Atty. Gen. 95, 2003 WL 21672836 (Cal.A.G.).

41. West's Ann.Cal.Gov.Code, sec. 20090.

42. *Wall Street Journal*, editorial, "CalPERS and Cronyism," October 18, 2004, A18.

43. Ibid., editorial, October 22, 2004, A16.

44. Ibid., editorial, August 20, 2004, A12.

45. Weinberg, "Sanctimonious in Sacramento," 52, 54. See also *Wall Street Journal*, "CalPERS and Cronyism" (containing numerous other examples of the CalPERS board's political "cronyism").

46. *Jackson v. Phillips*, 96 Mass. (14 Allen) 539, 579 (1867).

47. James J. Fishman, "Improving Charitable Accountability," *Maryland Law Review* 62 (2003): 218, 262.

48. California Prob. Code, sec. 15642 (West 1991).

49. See *Carl J. Herzog Foundation Inc. v. University of Bridgeport*, 243 Conn. 1, 699 A.2d 995 (1997).

50. *Perry v. United States*, 55 S.Ct. 432, 436 (1935).

51. *Bowen v. Gilliard*, 107 S.Ct. 3008, 3019 (1987).

52. *Helvering v. Davis; Flemming v. Nestor.*

53. 42 USCA s 401(a).

54. See *Lujan v. Defenders of Wildlife*, 504 U.S. 555 (1992), and *Raines v. Byrd*, 521 U.S. 811 (1997).

55. See, for example, *Palm Beach County Canvassing Board v. Harris*, 772 So.2d 1220 (Fla. 2000); *Carl J. Herzog Foundation v. University of Bridgeport*; and *Lockyer v. City and County of San Francisco*, 2004 WL 473257.

56. 1 Scott on Trusts, sec. 95 (1939).

57. *United States v. White Mountain Apache Tribe*, 123 S.Ct. 1126, 1131–1132 (2003).

58. *Wall Street Journal*, "Indian Takers," February 23, 1999, A22.

59. See generally Rounds, *Loring*, sec. 9.8.2, n. 25 and accompanying text.

60. It presumably could do so. Congress, for example, has bestowed on private citizens the right to bring actions under the federal False Claims Act. See *Vermont Agency of Natural Resources v. United States*, 529 U.S. 765 (2000).

61. See generally *Lynch v. United States*.

62. See, for example, *Hodel v. Irving*, 481 U.S. 704 (1987).

63. See, for example, *Minor v. United States*, 396 U.S. 87, 98 n. 13 (1969).

64. See Rounds, *Loring*, sec. 6.1.3.4, n. 168 (discussing an initiative of the Department of Labor to "encourage" private pension trustees to invest in economically targeted investments).

4

The Strategic Use of
Socially Responsible Investing

Jarol B. Manheim

*To date, corporate accountability activists have been very successful
at disrupting corporate rule. The task now must be to dismantle
corporate rule. If the goal is to redraw the balance of power between
society and big business, the corporate accountability movement
needs to focus on removing the sources of corporate authority. . . .
A first step would be to rewrite the charter laws to require broader
participation on corporate boards. Workers, consumers, shareholders, company suppliers, and local community leaders should all have
a voice on company boards. . . .*

*We must redesign the corporation's internal logic and refocus
its obligation to society at large, not just shareholders.*

—Kevin Danaher and Jason Mark[1]

*If "socialism" is defined as "ownership of the means of production
by the workers"—and this is both the orthodox and the only
rigorous definition—then the United States is the first truly
"Socialist" country.*

—Peter F. Drucker[2]

Anticorporate activism is now a commonplace of public life in the
United States and globally. It can be understood at many levels and
through many lenses—sociological, anthropological, political, and
economic, to name but a few. Central to any understanding of this

phenomenon is its dynamism. Anticorporate activism is fundamentally change-oriented. Its objective is to challenge and then change the behaviors of corporations. For that reason, there is value in examining such activism in the context of those factors that contribute to both stability and change in corporate behavior. When we apply this perspective, we find that anticorporate activism is essentially a political game—it is about power—and that the corporation per se, as a social institution, as well as the corporate–capitalist economy to which it gives rise and from which it derives its own legitimacy and standing, are both very much in play.

Balancing the Corporate Books

Most economists and business scholars define the corporation primarily as an economic entity—a mechanism for producing goods or services and maximizing profits. But suppose that we begin from the different premise that a corporation is a social institution whose purpose is to balance sets of sometimes reinforcing and often contradictory interests with diverse goals, only some of which are economic. Where the interests of these corporate stakeholders are sufficiently aligned, or in balance, the corporation will succeed in the marketplace, defend its interests in the polity, and contribute to the advancement of society in ways consistent with the objectives of its particular stakeholders. Where they fall out of alignment, pressure will be generated on the corporation to restore the previous state of balance—that is, to change its behaviors. The greater the degree of imbalance that is introduced—whether in the form of negative product claims, allegations of management misdeeds, class-action litigation, or other information that has the potential to undermine stakeholder confidence—the greater will be the pressure on the company to change its behavior in a way calculated to restore its reputation, independence, economic power, profitability, legitimacy, and the like to a balanced state.

This notion of corporate balance is a variant of the so-called "stakeholder theory" of the corporation, advanced by William Evan and Edward Freeman, and developed by such scholars as Margaret Blair and Lynn Stout.[3] But where that approach has generally been employed by advocates of "socially responsible investing" (SRI) to define and argue the importance of ethical behavior in business,[4] here the theory has a different application: identifying and leveraging fulcra where pressure can be efficiently applied to force changes in corporate policy, and through them, collectively, more general changes in public policy. This is a well-established strategy that was employed, for example, by the American civil rights movement of the 1950s and '60s and the antiapartheid movement of the 1970s and '80s.[5] Both the relationships between the corporation and its stakeholders, as such, and the thematic appeal of SRI rhetoric as applied in the context of those relationships, can provide leverage points.

Influential actors within the SRI community have systematically exploited these leverage points in order, first, to generate an imbalance in stakeholder relationships sufficient to require action on the part of a targeted company and, second, to channel corporate efforts at restoring balance, whether through public positioning or behavior change, toward outcomes regarded by that community as desirable. It is not necessary (nor do I argue) that SRI advocates have consciously applied this balance theory per se, but only that imposing the theory on the data provided by their actions helps us to understand the dynamics of influence in this increasingly important arena. The main elements of the argument include the application of power structure analysis, the advancement of systemic changes in shareholders' rights, the waging of proxy battles over corporate governance and social policy, and the integration of this effort in the form of a "social netwar." To the extent such efforts are effective in the aggregate, broad changes in the character, functioning, standing, and impact of the corporation as a social institution will follow, with both intended and unintended consequences.

Power Structure Analysis:
A Pathology of Stakeholder Relationships

As long ago as the 1970s, selected unions and the progenitors of today's generation of anticorporate activists developed a methodology for analyzing corporations and assessing their various strengths and vulnerabilities. The objective of these early corporate antagonists, such as the North American Congress on Latin America and the Amalgamated Clothing and Textile Workers Union, was to attack corporations at their roots by disrupting the stakeholder relationships upon which they depended for everything from their daily business routines to their basic standing in society. They termed this methodology "power structure analysis," and developed a virtual library of guidebooks on how to conduct and exploit research on target companies.[6] A labor activist who rose to prominence during this period, Ray Rogers, applied the technique to union organizing at J. P. Stevens and elsewhere, and helped to initiate the phenomenon known as the corporate, or anticorporate, campaign.[7]

As illustrated in figure 1, power structure analysis places the corporation at the center of an array of stakeholders upon whose support or goodwill it depends. One then examines each of the resulting relationships, sets them against one's own strengths, weaknesses, and resources, and develops a prioritized order of attack against the target company. The objective of this attack may be labor related (for example, organizing workers), policy related (forcing a change in the company's environmental sensitivities), or power related (challenging the legitimacy, autonomy, or influence of the company).

The attack itself then follows, with the intent of disrupting the established balance among the stakeholders. It might take the form of a challenge to the company on a human rights issue, causing shifts in its relationships with the faith community, civil libertarians, or the media. It might be a challenge to the company's workplace policies, generating pressure on its relationship with its employees or with selected regulators. It might challenge the company's faithfulness to the law, putting pressure on its relationship with legislators and the courts. Or, as but one among many more such options, it might take the form of a challenge to the legitimacy and responsiveness of the company's internal governance norms and practices as indicative of poor corporate ethics and citizenship, thereby putting strain on its relationships with a wide range of stakeholders, but, most notably, with its regulators and selected institutional shareholders.

FIGURE 1

SELECTED CORPORATE STAKEHOLDER RELATIONSHIPS
USED IN POWER STRUCTURE ANALYSIS

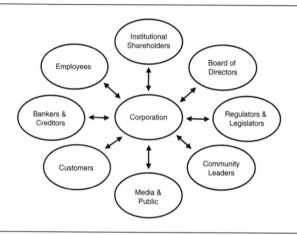

SOURCE: Based on Jarol B. Manheim, *The Death of a Thousand Cuts: Corporate Campaigns and the Attack on the Corporation* (Mahwah, N.J.: Lawrence Erlbaum Associates, 2001), 196.

The salient point regarding power structure analysis is that it resembles in every key way the sort of analysis one might produce in pursuit of the so-called stakeholder theory of the corporation. The only difference is that, rather than purporting to maximize the contribution of the corporation to some broadened affirmative social agenda, the analysis is conducted with a specific, anticorporate objective in mind.

Yet, in context, it is this very difference that provides an essential strategic opportunity for anticorporate activists. Put most simply, though many Americans have clear and historical reservations about the role and practices of major corporations, and though those reservations have been recently brought to the fore by a well-documented series of transgressions by such companies as Enron and WorldCom, it is unlikely that most or even many people would subscribe to an agenda that called for disrupting, let alone dismantling, the very companies that provide them with jobs, goods, and services. They might, however, rise to a *higher* calling that emphasized good corporate governance, corporate responsiveness to shareholders and other stakeholder communities, and, above all, corporate social responsibility.

In strategic terms, then, a fundamentally *anticorporate* movement that could weld itself onto the thematic appeals of less extreme corporate reformers could, potentially, achieve a far higher degree of public acceptance and influence than it could on its own. In this way, responsible reformers could be used to legitimize and provide cover for the anticorporate movement. At the same time, those more moderate reformers could enhance the visibility and effectiveness of their own efforts, and build their power base, through the same alliances. And since it would be their own moral and rhetorical frames that would dominate the discourse, moderate reformers could participate in such alliances at minimal risk to their own credibility, at least in the near term.

Anticorporate Activists and Public Pension Funds

Central to constructing such an alliance would be redefining the mechanisms of influence to facilitate cooperation among these sets of interests. In particular, a rationale would need to be developed that would permit institutional shareholders, and most particularly the trustees of pension funds that control a significant proportion of publicly traded equities, to act upon a new agenda of corporate reform: incorporating both governance practices and social issues without violating their fiduciary responsibilities.

Why would the pension funds play so critical a role? From 1970 to the present, organized labor, environmental and human rights activists, and others have conducted hundreds of systematic campaigns to pressure corporations to alter one or another of their policies. Despite some successes, these campaigns have not brought about a widespread change in corporate behavior. They have failed for the simple reason that they have not exercised sufficient leverage on many of the targeted companies to force such changes.[8] Many companies have been damaged, to be sure, by the attacks on their reputations, the litigation, the regulatory proceedings, and the like that are so much a part of anticorporate campaigns. Yet, on the whole, the number and size of the companies that dominate the economy so far exceed the resources the activists have been able to mobilize against them as to render them relatively invulnerable.

There are exceptions: Publicly held companies do listen to their major shareholders, many of which are institutions. And among the largest, and therefore most influential, institutional shareholders are the multiemployer union pension funds and the public-employee pension funds. As of 1999, the last year for which complete data are available, the private multiemployer (or so-called Taft-Hartley) funds and the public-employee pension funds together controlled approximately $3 *trillion* of investments. Some of this money is invested in debt and some in equities, but in recent years both the aggregate amount and the proportion of their investments in equities have grown substantially. The Conference Board reports, for example, that between 1980 and 2001, the proportion of pension-fund assets allocated to equities in the United States increased from 35 percent to 51 percent. The shift was led by state and local public-employee funds, which more than doubled their commitment to equities, from 23 percent of their rapidly growing portfolios in 1980 to 56 percent in 2001. (In absolute terms, public-employee funds actually increased their equity holdings 2,700 percent, from $44 billion to $1.2 trillion, during this period.)[9] In corporate democracy, shares are votes, and these funds have a great many shares.

But as critical as their potential role might be in advancing an SRI agenda, the trustees of these pension funds are both morally and legally obligated to invest, and to vote the shares in the companies in which they invest, in the best interests of their beneficiaries—that is, to exercise fiduciary responsibility. And, traditionally, fiduciary responsibility has been defined as supporting policies and actions that advance the financial well-being of the beneficiaries. Historically, this has led pension funds and similar investors to be among the strongest supporters of management at companies with solid earnings. Indeed, by some interpretations, such fiduciaries could not take any other type of results into account in their decision making. If the activists were to mobilize the latent power of these holdings, they had to address this problem.

They have done that at three levels. First, they set out to demonstrate that SRI was not fiscally irresponsible. They have cited numerous, if conflicting, academic studies and reports prepared for the Social Investment Forum—the SRI industry trade group—that compared the performance of two leading indexes of socially screened mutual funds, the Domini Social Index and the Citizens' Index, with that of the Standard & Poor's 500 Index. At least some of these studies purport to show that the two specialized indexes matched or exceeded the performance of the overall market during a selected time frame.[10] Such results would suggest that fund managers could meet their fiduciary responsibility, even under the traditional definition, using selected social-investing screens.[11]

Second, they set out to change the traditional definition of fiduciary responsibility. For example, in 1998, the AFL-CIO adopted new proxy voting guidelines for trustees of private, multiemployer pension funds. These guidelines explicitly endorsed as consistent with trustees' fiduciary responsibility the advancement and support of shareholder resolutions relating to the reform of corporate governance and the corporate pursuit of social policy objectives, *even if these changes appeared to have a negative impact on the near-term financial performance of a given company.* The rationale offered was that companies that better served their communities by enhancing their environmental, health and safety, labor relations, and other policies were serving the interests of fund beneficiaries in ways that, albeit not financial in character, were nonetheless real.[12] As restated in the 2003 edition of the guidelines, the federation advised:

> The duties of loyalty and prudence require the voting fiduciary to make voting decisions consistent with the "economic best interests" of plan participants and beneficiaries; this does not mean that the voting fiduciary is required to maximize short-term gains if such a decision

is not consistent with the long-term economic best interest of the participants and beneficiaries.[13]

Third, to facilitate the direct consideration of a far broader range of issues, activists set out to change the rules under which corporations customarily dealt with shareholder resolutions. In determining which of the many and varied unsolicited resolutions they must convey to shareholders for a vote, companies are guided by Securities and Exchange Commission (SEC) rule 14a-8, which establishes the criteria for inclusion in the company's proxy materials. Before 1998, the SEC routinely allowed companies to exclude many resolutions that dealt with workplace-related social issues, such as the environment. But in May 1998, following a campaign in which it received more than 2,000 letters from activists, the SEC changed the rule to require that a much wider range of resolutions, if advanced, must be included in the annual proxy solicitation.[14]

These and other similar initiatives designed to set the stewards of these vast pension resources free to pursue a social and political agenda have been accompanied by a parallel effort to pressure other fiduciaries, most notably the mutual-fund industry, to do the same. In 2003, the AFL-CIO launched a "transparency" campaign to push Fidelity Investments and others in the industry to report their proxy voting positions to their own investors on the assumption this would increase the likelihood of fund managers to support positions framed by activists as "pro-social." This campaign produced its first fruit in 2004.

Activist shareholders, some of whom are notorious gadflies, have been advancing resolutions for many years. And under the revised rule 14a-8, a diverse set of such proposals has moved to votes at thousands of companies. Among the issues brought forward have been workplace codes of conduct, environmental reporting requirements, the abandonment of lines of business, use of genetic engineering, transparency in corporate political contributions, and doing business in China, to name a few.

But the real action in the past three or four years, which has drawn together the combination of ideologically motivated activists, pension-fund managers, and trustees with whom we are most directly concerned here, is more organic in character, focusing not on social policies, but on corporate governance, and more specifically on changes to structures and processes that will, over time, further enhance the power of these selfsame shareholders. Having begun with a campaign to reduce and restrict the forms of executive compensation—an issue on which corporate critics were easily able to muster media, public, and political support—this effort has now moved on to a matter of far greater importance: the functioning of the corporation. It includes such elements as:

- cumulative voting for directors, which allows pooling of votes for a small number of outside candidates;

- a requirement that two candidates be nominated for each board position, guaranteeing the opportunity to oust directors who resist the reform agenda;

- declassification of the board, which refers to single-year rather than staggered terms of office. This means the entire board is up for reelection annually and therefore potentially more sensitive to reform influences;

- splitting the roles of chairman of the board and chief executive officer, thus dividing power within the corporation and weakening management;

- a requirement that directors receive a majority of affirmative votes to be elected to the board—another mechanism to increase responsiveness to institutional shareholders;

- establishment of a shareholders committee to negotiate with a board of directors that fails to implement resolutions approved by a majority vote;

- a requirement that companies hire advisory firms—the same ones that advise or even lead the reform movement—to advise their shareholders how to vote on management-initiated resolutions.

As part of this effort to open the boardroom to dissident voices, in 2003 activists pressed the SEC to adopt a rule requiring that in certain circumstances institutional shareholders of some standing could nominate their own candidates for corporate directorships. For its part, the AFL-CIO argued that such a change would level the playing field for institutional investors. The federation's petition to the commission stated in part:

> Granting institutional shareholders the ability to economically run independent candidates for boards of directors is a key response to both the broader corporate crisis and the specific longstanding problem of corporate boards ignoring investor concerns. . . .
>
> Under the current director election process, shareholders vote only on candidates nominated by the directors themselves. Although state law permits shareholders to run their own candidates, in reality this only occurs at public companies in the rare event of a hostile takeover given the tremendous cost of proxy fights. These costs are prohibitive even for the largest institutional investors given their diverse portfolios. With no meaningful ability to cost effectively run directors, or to even vote against incumbent directors, shareholders can do little more than rubberstamp a company's nominees. For shareholders, this inevitably results in an inability to hold directors accountable for their performance and an extreme reliance on government regulation and oversight.[15]

Other advocates offered similar arguments. As of this writing, the proposed regulation to this effect is still pending.

It is small wonder that the public pension funds have coalesced around this agenda, for it clearly serves to enhance their influence on the nation's largest corporations. And, in fact, many elements of the reform agenda are reasonable on their face when they are employed primarily as safeguards against abuse. Therein lie their appeal and their potency. But it must also be understood that, in the process of advancing this reform agenda, more moderate reformers also advance the interests of their less visible allies, the anticorporate activists, with whom at least some, but not all, of the pension-fund decision makers share common cause. And it is here that the danger lies, for the very same measures that can facilitate needed reform at some corporations can themselves be abused by coalitions of likeminded anticorporate campaigners, for whom they create a new source of power.

This beyond-reform coalition building has been facilitated domestically through such organizations as the Council of Institutional Investors (CII) and, especially, the National Coalition for Corporate Reform (NCCR).

CII was established in 1985, and today numbers among its members 130 pension funds, predominantly union-based and state-employee funds, with collective assets of more than $3 trillion. Another 125 partners include some of the prime movers of the governance reform movement, such as Hermes Pensions Management Limited and Institutional Shareholder Services.[16] Through conferences and other activities, the organization plays a central role in shaping reform initiatives favored by its largely pro-labor membership, which is to say, advancing the principles set out in the AFL-CIO's guidelines; and, by virtue of its name and market power, it legitimizes even the definitions of terms around which the debate over governance is conducted. A number of shareholder resolutions explicitly cite CII positions or definitions as a rationale for support on such matters as the independence of directors.

NCCR, established in 2003, consists of about a dozen public-employee pension funds as well as two unions, the Service Employees International Union (SEIU) and the American Federation of State, County and Municipal Employees (AFSCME), and the Amalgamated Bank (also known as UNITE HERE, the textile- and hotel-workers union). Though smaller in size and looser in organization, NCCR is far more aggressive in its actions than CII. Even as its creation was announced by the New York State comptroller at the annual CII conference in that year, with explicit backing from AFL-CIO president John Sweeney, it was clear that NCCR attracted only

FIGURE 2

**MEMBERSHIP IN THE COUNCIL OF INSTITUTIONAL INVESTORS AND
THE NATIONAL COALITION FOR CORPORATE REFORM, 2004**

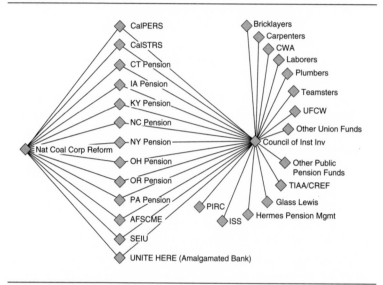

SOURCE: Based on CII membership lists posted at www.cii.org (accessed May 17, 2004), and on NCCR membership, as listed in Mary Williams Walsh and Jonathan D. Glater, "Pension Fund Trustees Taking Aim at Safeway," *New York Times*, March 26, 2004. Prepared using S. P. Borgatti, M. G. Everett, and L. C. Freeman, *Ucinet for Windows: Software for Social Network Analysis*, Version 6.12 (Harvard: Analytic Technologies, 2002).

the most activist of members.[17] The pension funds and state officials who have been most aggressive in pursuing reform at such companies as Citicorp, Disney, and Safeway are all associated with NCCR.

Figure 2 shows some of the pension funds or related unions represented in CII and NCCR, respectively. Connecting lines in the figure represent direct membership or, in the case of the AFL-CIO and NCCR, explicit endorsement of the creation of the organization. Principal among those with dual participation are CalPERS, whose board of directors has been controlled by such unions as the United Food and Commercial Workers (UFCW), the Laborers, and the

SEIU, and whose policies are greatly influenced by activist state treasurer Phil Angelides, and the pension funds of New York and Connecticut, each of which is also influenced by activist state officials with close ties to organized labor.

Proxy Wars and "Social Netwars"

The battles over corporate governance structures and social policies are but the most public manifestations of an underlying struggle for economic and political power that pits the newly invigorated "progressive" movement against corporate America. That larger struggle is commonly channeled through a variety of alliance structures, including one devoted to waging proxy warfare.

In their pathbreaking work, *Activists Beyond Borders*, Margaret E. Keck and Kathryn Sikkink posited what they termed a "boomerang model" of NGO influence.[18] In it, a nongovernmental organization (NGO) that lacks sufficient ability to affect policy in its own respective domestic system can work through international coalitions with partners who are better able to influence political actors in other nations or in international governmental organizations (IGOs). Using such mechanisms as international treaty or trade negotiations, these sovereign or semisovereign actors can then be mobilized to pressure the government of the NGO's nation to change its policies. The dynamics of this activity revolve around four major political axes: information, symbols, leverage, and accountability.[19]

An equally important volume, *Networks and Netwars*, built on Sikkink's earlier work to provide a regime-based view of the same phenomenon, which editors John Arquilla and David Ronfeldt have termed "social netwar."[20] A social netwar is, in their terms,

> characterized by militant activists operating in, and as . . . issue networks. . . . A social netwar is likely to involve battles for public opinion and for media access and coverage, at local through global levels. It is also likely to revolve around propaganda campaigns, psychological

warfare, and strategic [communication], not just to edu-
cate and inform, but to deceive and disinform as well.[21]

Social netwars, and the activist networks that engage in them,
need not be international in character; the same concept can have
wholly domestic analogues. Nor are their targets necessarily nation-
states or even explicitly political actors; they could, for example,
just as easily include corporations. Indeed, it does not require a
great stretch of the imagination to characterize the network of
activist pension funds, their efforts to establish and leverage legitimacy for their reform agenda, their framing of the corporate governance debate in terms of accountability and corporate social
responsibility, and their literal swarming of their corporate targets
as precisely such an exercise.

That said, it is, in fact, possible in the present instance to discern
as well an international network of pension-fund and pension-fund-
related activists. Figure 3 identifies some of the protagonists in this
network and *some* of the membership links and interconnections
among them.

The International Institutional Investors Advisory Group, one of
two principal international nodes in this network, was established
in March 1999 for the stated purpose of transforming country-
specific, corporate governance guidelines into a set of international
standards. Membership is limited to the four organizations shown.[22]
The International Corporate Governance Network was founded in
1995 at the initiative of CalPERS, which later joined with the UFCW
in hosting its 1998 annual conference. This group, too, is devoted to
developing international standards of corporate governance.[23] In a
letter dated April 15, 2004, Alistair Ross Goobey, chairman of the
ICGN board of governors, announced to the membership a plan to
increase the public visibility and influence of the organization.

Goobey is a key player who also heads up Hermes Pensions
Management Limited, the owned and operated management arm
of the British Telecom and British Post Office pension schemes.
Hermes, in turn, financed the most recent change in ownership of
Institutional Shareholder Services (ISS), which is the primary U.S.

Figure 3
Selected International Pension Fund Network Interlocks

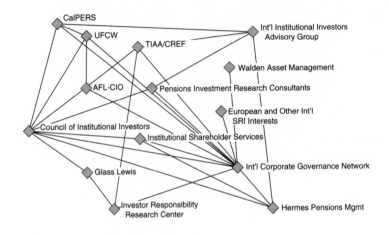

Source: Based on the summary of members and their roles found at www.icgn.org/history.html on May 17, 2004 (since removed) and at www.icgn.org, November 1, 2004. Prepared using S. P. Borgatti, M. G. Everett, and L. C. Freeman, *Ucinet for Windows: Software for Social Network Analysis*, Version 6.12 (Harvard: Analytic Technologies, 2002).

proxy advisory service for institutional investors, and is represented on the Institutional Shareholder Services board. (Robert Monks, who is now deputy director of Hermes, formed ISS some years ago. His son, Robert C. S. Monks, now chairs the ISS board.) Until December 2004, a representative of the UFCW chaired the board of CalPERS. Teachers Insurance and Annuity Association/ College Retirement Equities Fund (TIAA/CREF) is represented on the board of the Investor Responsibility Research Center, which has partnered with the investment advisory firm of Glass Lewis to enter competition with ISS in the proxy-advising business.

The result of all this networking is a collection of interconnected actors operating with a measure of coordination, but with a decentralized leadership, to legitimize one another and impose an international regime of governance standards on U.S. (and other) corporations through proxy battles and other means.

An example of this networking in action is found in what we might think of as the corporate governance "issue of the year" for 2004, the splitting of the roles of chief executive officer and chairman of the board, with the latter required to be a director with no current or recent role in a given company's management. The AFL-CIO announced at the beginning of the 2004 proxy season that it intended to introduce, through unions and union pension funds, resolutions calling for this reform at approximately fifty companies. Only about twenty of the companies listed in the Standard & Poors 500 and only seven of the largest two hundred fifty among them follow this practice.[24] In contrast, in the United Kingdom this division of roles is incorporated in the Common Code of Practice—the basic business law—and approximately 90 percent of all firms have adopted it. Those that have not are required to explain their decision to shareholders. The relationship between the CEO and chair, then, is one on which U.S. and European practices differ dramatically, and where a network of labor-based institutional shareholders is in the process of trying to impose the European standard on numerous American corporations.

Conclusion

By reconceptualizing the corporation as a social entity about which the interests of various stakeholders are balanced, and by considering the impact on the corporation of an imbalance introduced by an (anticorporate) antagonist, we could enrich our understanding of the strategies of the SRI movement. The "reform" agenda advanced by SRI advocates and their activist allies is designed to weaken the ability of corporate management and corporate directors to make decisions independent of shareholder pressure. That is clearly the thrust of the more significant corporate governance resolutions introduced in recent years; and, in the abstract, such reforms appear to be democratic and appropriate, precisely as they are characterized by the media and parts of the academic community.

However, it should be recognized that these activist shareholders are not individual nor disorganized institutional shareholders, but rather the major investors who are most effectively organized to coordinate their actions—most notably, the unions and the public-employee pension funds. Indeed, they are the principal architects of the network of shareholder activists. To the extent that corporations are forced to adopt governance changes limiting management independence and enhancing "responsiveness," it is to the unions and their allies that power will shift. If successful, this shift in power and influence is likely to produce over time a fundamentally different style of business in the United States, which may prove more socially responsible by some standards and quite probably less competitive in the global marketplace (since the globalization of governance standards will "equalize" business practices, and may do so at the expense of the successful American model), or both.

Therein lies the principal irony of this phenomenon, for if U.S. corporations become less competitive, they will likely become less profitable and perhaps less able to sustain high levels of employment. In the first instance, the value and yield of United States–based equities—the very shares that the pension funds are leveraging for influence in annual meetings—will decline, thereby reducing the financial well-being of the beneficiaries whose interests these funds are charged with protecting. In the second instance, there will be fewer and fewer union jobs upon which to sustain either a pension plan or a viable labor movement. As the responsibility for consequently underfunded public pension funds shifts to taxpayers, those who are employed will bear an ever-greater burden.

At that point in time, corporate imbalance may have been reduced—and some new balance achieved—but perhaps at the expense of greater economic and political imbalance. And as that point nears, it may be the fault lines *within* today's alliance of convenience among SRI advocates and anticorporate ideological advocacy groups that come under pressure and are tested.

Notes

1. Kevin Danaher and Jason Mark, *Insurrection: Citizen Challenges to Corporate Power* (New York: Routledge, 2003), 299–302.

2. Peter F. Drucker, *The Unseen Revolution: How Pension Fund Socialism Came to America* (New York: Harper & Row, 1976), 1.

3. William M. Evan and R. Edward Freeman, "A Stakeholder Theory of the Modern Corporation: Kantian Capitalism," in *Ethical Theory and Business*, ed. Tom L. Beauchamp and Norman Bowie (Englewood Cliffs, N.J.: Prentice-Hall, 1993), 97–106. See also, for example, Margaret M. Blair and Lynn A. Stout, "Director Accountability and the Mediating Role of the Corporate Board," working paper series in business economics and regulatory law, working paper no. 266622, Georgetown University Law Center, 2001.

4. A case in point is Margaret M. Blair, "Shareholder Value, Corporate Governance and Corporate Performance: A Post-Enron Reassessment of the Conventional Wisdom," in *Corporate Governance and Capital Flows in a Global Economy*, ed. Peter K. Cornelius and Bruce Kogut (New York: Oxford University Press, 2003).

5. For an excellent analysis of these earlier applications, see David Vogel, *Lobbying the Corporation: Citizen Challenges to Business Authority* (New York: Basic Books, 1978).

6. The oldest of these was the *NACLA Research Methodology Guide*, produced by the North American Congress on Latin America (New York, 1970). This particular guide also included chapters on infiltrating or otherwise using to advantage such social institutions as labor unions and churches.

7. Jarol B. Manheim, *The Death of a Thousand Cuts: Corporate Campaigns and the Attack on the Corporation* (Mahwah, N.J.: Lawrence Erlbaum Associates, 2001), 51–57.

8. On these campaigns and their failures see, for example, Jarol B. Manheim, *Biz-War and the Out-of-Power Elite: The Progressive Left Attack on the Corporation* (Mahwah, N.J.: Lawrence Erlbaum Associates, 2004), and Donald H. Schepers and S. Prakash Sethi, "Do Socially Responsible Funds Actually Deliver What They Promise? Bridging the Gap Between the Promise and Performance of Socially Responsible Funds," *Business and Society Review* 108, no. 1 (2003): 11–32.

9. Based on data reported in *Institutional Investment Report: Equity Ownership and Investment Strategies of U.S. and International Institutional Investors* (New York: Conference Board, May 2002), and in *Institutional Investment Report: Financial Assets and Equity Holdings—Patterns of*

Institutional Investment and Control (New York: Conference Board, March 2003); and on data provided to the author by the Employee Benefit Security Administration of the U.S. Department of Labor.

10. Social Investment Forum, *1999 Report on Socially Responsible Investing Trends in the United States* (Washington, D.C.: SIF Industry Research Program, 1999), Figure 6.

11. Jon Entine, however, calls into question the methodology on which this argument is based—*and* the research criteria employed by SR funds to select investment vehicles—in "The Myth of Social Investing: A Critique of Its Practice and Consequences for Corporate Social Performance Research," *Organization and Environment* 20, no. 10 (September 2003): 1–17.

12. AFL-CIO, *Investing in Our Future: AFL-CIO Proxy Voting Guidelines* (Washington, D.C.: AFL-CIO, 1998).

13. Ibid.; *Exercising Authority, Restoring Accountability: The AFL-CIO Proxy Voting Guidelines* (Washington, D.C.: AFL-CIO, 2003), 2.

14. Cynthia J. Campbell, Stuart L. Gillan, and Cathy M. Niden, "Current Perspectives on Shareholder Proposals: Lessons from the 1997 Proxy Season," *Financial Management* 28, no. 1 (March 22, 1999): 89.

15. Correspondence from Richard L. Trumka, AFL-CIO secretary-treasurer, to Jonathan G. Katz, secretary of the SEC, May 15, 2003.

16. From the membership list of the Council of Institutional Investors, found online at www.cii.org/dcwascii/web.nsf/doc/about_index.cm (accessed May 13, 2004).

17. Patrick McGeehan, "Big Investors Urged to Unite for Reforms," *New York Times*, September 4, 2003, C8.

18. Margaret E. Keck and Kathryn Sikkink, *Activists Beyond Borders: Advocacy Networks in International Politics* (Ithaca, N.Y.: Cornell University Press, 1998).

19. Ibid., 16.

20. John Arquilla and David Ronfeldt, eds., *Networks and Netwars: The Future of Terror, Crime and Militancy* (Santa Monica, Calif.: RAND, 2001).

21. David Ronfeldt, John Arquilla, Graham E. Fuller, and Melissa Fuller, *The Zapatista Social Netwar in Mexico* (Santa Monica, Calif.: RAND, 1998), 20–22.

22. Richard Donkin, "Powerful Support for International Guidelines," *Financial Times*, March 19, 1999, 4.

23. This objective is set forth in "ICGN Founding Principles," http://www.icgn.org/documents/ICGN-founding-principles.html (accessed May 17, 2004).

24. Based on data reported in "Governance Research from the Corporate Library—Split CEO/Chairman Roles—March 2004," www.thecorporate library.com (accessed May 16, 2004).

About the Authors

Jon Entine is a scholar in residence at Miami University (Ohio) and an adjunct fellow at the American Enterprise Institute, writing on science and public policy and corporate social responsibility. His recent works include *Dangerous Liaisons: Why Social Investing Threatens Public Employee Pension Funds and the Social Security Trust Fund*, ed. Robert Kolb (2006); *Let Them Eat Precaution: How Politics Is Undermining the Genetic Revolution in Agriculture* (2006); "Socially Responsible Business," in *The Encyclopedia of Leadership*, ed. Georgia Sorenson and James MacGregor Burns (2004); "The Stranger-Than-Truth Story of the Body Shop," in *Killed: Great Journalism Too Hot to Print*, ed. David Wallis (2004); and "The Politics of Brent Spar: Shell vs. Greenpeace," in *Case Histories in Business Ethics: The Virtues and Moral Decision Making in Business*, ed. Chris Megone and Simon Robinson (2002). Before launching his writing career, Entine was a network television news producer, winning more than twenty awards, including two Emmys for specials on the reform movements in China and the former Soviet Union. In 1989, Entine produced and cowrote with Tom Brokaw the documentary *Black Athletes: Fact and Fiction* (named Best International Sports Film of 1989), which provided the inspiration for Entine's book *Taboo: Why Black Athletes Dominate Sports and Why We're Afraid to Talk about It* (2000). Entine has taught at various universities, including Columbia, Michigan, Arizona State, New York University, and Miami University.

Jarol B. Manheim is a professor of media and public affairs and of political science at the George Washington University, where he was the founding director of the School of Media and Public Affairs. His research in strategic political communication has appeared in the leading journals of political science, journalism, and mass communication. Among his books are *Biz-War and the "Out-of-Power Elite": The Progressive Left Attack on the Corporation* (2004); *The Death of a Thousand Cuts: Corporate Campaigns and the Attack on the Corporation* (2001); *Corporate Conduct Unbecoming: Codes of Conduct and Anti-Corporate Strategy* (2000); and *Strategic Public Diplomacy and American Foreign Policy: The Evolution of Influence* (1994). Manheim has addressed the senior staff of the U.S. Department of Labor on corporate campaigns and related topics and the Secretary's Open Forum of the Department of State on the use of strategic communication in public diplomacy. He has also lectured on strategic communication at the National Defense University; testified before Congress on corporate campaigns; and addressed business leaders, attorneys, and trade and professional associations across the United States in a variety of forums. He is the past chair of the political communication section of the American Political Science Association, and in 1995 he was selected as the District of Columbia Professor of the Year by the Council for the Advancement and Support of Education and the Carnegie Foundation for the Advancement of Teaching. He is also a recipient of the McGannon Award for Social and Ethical Relevance in Communication Research.

Alicia H. Munnell is the Peter F. Drucker Professor of Management Sciences and director of the Center for Retirement Research at the Boston College Carroll School of Management. She was cofounder and first president of the National Academy of Social Insurance and is currently a member of the American Academy of Arts and Sciences, the Institute of Medicine, the National Academy of Public Administration, and the Pension Research Council at Wharton. She is a member of the boards of the Wheeling-Pittsburgh Steel Corporation, the Century Foundation, the National Bureau of Economic Research, and the Pension Rights Center. She has published many articles and books and has edited several volumes on tax policy, Social Security, public and private pensions, and productivity. Her works include *The Oxford Handbook of Pensions and Retirement Income* (with Gordon Clark and Michael Orzag, forthcoming 2005); *Coming Up Short: The Challenge of 401(k) Plans* (with Annika Sundén, 2004); *Death and*

Dollars: The Role of Gifts and Bequests in America (with Annika Sundén, 2003); *Framing the Social Security Debate: Values, Politics and Economics* (with R. Douglas Arnold and Michael Graetz, 1998); *The Economics of Private Pensions* (1982); and *The Future of Social Security* (1977). She has served on the President's Council of Economic Advisers (1995–97) as assistant secretary of the Treasury for economic policy (1993–95), and as an economist, senior vice president, and director of research at the Federal Reserve Bank of Boston.

Charles E. Rounds Jr., a professor of law at Suffolk University Law School specializing in agency and trust law, is a fellow of the American College of Trust and Estate Counsel, a member of the Advisory Committee of the Cato Project on Social Security Choice, and a resident fellow of the Beacon Hill Institute. He has been the author since 1994 of *Loring: A Trustee's Handbook*, which was first published in 1898. Rounds has also authored two papers on Social Security for the Cato Institute: *Property Rights: The Hidden Issue of Social Security Reform* (2000) and *A Proposed Legal, Regulatory, and Operational Structure for an Investment-Based Social Security System* (with Karl J. Borden, 2002). He serves as an expert witness and consultant in fiduciary litigation around the country. He is also onsite coordinator of Suffolk's summer law program at the University of Lund in Sweden. In 1995, he testified on economically targeted investments before the Joint Economic Committee of Congress. Prior to that, he was counsel to the Franklin Foundation, by statute sole managing agent of a now-terminated, two-hundred-year accumulation trust established under the will of Benjamin Franklin.

Annika Sundén is a senior economist at the Social Insurance Agency in Stockholm and a research associate at the Center for Retirement Research. She was previously an economist at the Federal Reserve Board in Washington, D.C., where she was involved in the design and implementation of the Survey of Consumer Finances. Sundén is also a member of the National Academy of Social Insurance. Her recent publications include *Coming Up Short: The Challenge of 401(k) Plans* (with Alicia H. Munnell, 2004); *Death and Dollars: The Role of Gifts and*

Bequests in America (with Alicia H. Munnell, 2003); *Portfolio Choice, Trading and Returns in a Large 401(k) Plan* (with Julie Agnew and Pierluigi Balduzzi, 2000); and *How Will Sweden's New Pension System Work?* (2000).

Index